OBEDIENCE AND SECURITY TRAINING
FOR DOGS

The author with his dog Nelson

OBEDIENCE AND SECURITY TRAINING FOR DOGS

TOM SCOTT

Formerly of the London Metropolitan Police Dog Section

ARCO PUBLISHING COMPANY, INC.
New York

Published by ARCO PUBLISHING COMPANY, INC.

219 Park Avenue South

New York, N.Y. 10003

★

Library of Congress Catalog Card Number 69–10326

ISBN 668–01786–4

All Rights Reserved

Third printing 1973

For
Edith

Contents

Illustrations

Throughout the text of this book, the German Shepherd dog is referred to as the 'Alsatian' dog.

Preface

My first introduction to the training of dogs was in early youth, when my ambition was to make a career of agriculture. With this object in view I obtained employment on a number of farms, where I became interested in the way animals were trained for various purposes. I was particularly impressed with the sagacity of sheep-dogs, their speed and nimbleness, and the assistance they gave to the farmer or shepherd in controlling sheep. Later, when training dogs for other purposes, the experience I had gained on farms stood me in good stead.

In 1929 I joined the Metropolitan Police and soon found that on night duty, especially in lonely districts, I was much happier when I had my Alsatian dog with me. On many occasions I came in contact with gypsies and similar types, where the presence of a dog commanded immediate respect and made my work in dealing with such people very much easier.

This was several years before police dogs were considered seriously. At that time it was thought very un-English to use dogs in this capacity, and it took a considerable amount of legislation before approval was given for trained police dogs and handlers to be appointed for criminal work. Public opinion had to be sounded, as well as decisions on the extent to which police dogs could be employed in the United Kingdom.

It was not until 1948 that dog patrols were introduced into the Metropolitan Police. I was one of those selected as a handler, and during the training of these newly acquired dogs I learnt a great deal, acquired much experience, and realised the impact that trained police dogs would have on criminals. I knew that dogs had been used with success for some forty years in Germany and that their training for police work had been very thorough, so I put forward the suggestion that we might be able to exchange ideas and obtain information from that country. The suggestion, however, was not taken up, although I often heard it repeated from other sources. The original police dog handlers had to pool their own ideas, and formulate their own methods of training and applying them to police work. Had they and their dogs not justified themselves, that would have been the end of police dogs, but fortunately they proved more successful than had been thought possible.

I handled the first police Alsatian, a bitch, and was naturally proud of her when she played a part in the arrest of a criminal, a fitting reward for us both after our strenuous period of training. I must add that we were given every possible encouragement to prove ourselves. Demonstrations were arranged at police colleges and at various public fêtes with the object of creating interest in the general public and to show the effectiveness of police dogs. These demonstrations were highly successful and, as a result, we had visitors from foreign and colonial police who adopted the methods of training that our original handlers had laid down and practised.

I remember one such demonstration that we gave to the Prefect of the Paris police and his lady, who were accompanied by the then Commissioner of Police and other high-ranking officers. A 'track' was laid for my Alsatian bitch Jill while my colleagues and I were engaged in giving the obedience part of the demonstration. When Jill had completed her track the senior officers standing around me were, I could see, well pleased with the dog's accomplishment, and the Prefect's lady was greatly impressed.

'Bravo, bravo!' she cried, and wanted to pat the dog's head, but I had made it a habit never to allow anyone to pet my dog until she was given what I called the 'password'. Without this, anyone who tried to pat the dog was rebuffed by vigorous barking. Actually, the password was a whisper from me, audible to the dog but inaudible to anyone standing a yard or two away. There were many unbelieving looks on the faces of my audience when I said to the lady, 'You will have to say the password, madam, before you may pat my dog,' but she smiled as if I were joking, and with the help of those around her, for her knowledge of English was not very extensive, she approached the dog and tried to coax it to be friendly. Jill, however, stood her ground, barked furiously, and the lady withdrew. Eventually she decided that I must, after all, be serious, and asked for the password.

'Madam,' I said, 'may I ask your name?'

A little surprised, she nevertheless gave it. 'Maria,' she said.

Banteringly I said, 'I hope that is correct, madam. If it isn't the dog will know.'

'It is correct,' she replied.

'Then,' I said, 'if you will say to her, "Dear Fifinella, my name is Maria," she will allow you to pat her.'

The lady, feeling a little foolish perhaps, nevertheless repeated my words, and Jill allowed herself to be patted, I having whispered to her to submit. A little later the lady wished to repeat the caress but Jill rebuffed her and I told her that she would have to repeat the password before Jill would respond to her advances. She did so, and Jill, responding to my whisper, again allowed the caress.

By now, all those who had witnessed the demonstration were convinced that Jill had amazing powers of discrimination. I have often used the methods described in this incident on men and women who have wanted to pat my dog.

This incident may seem a trivial, purposeless piece of trickery, but I do not believe in teaching dogs useless tricks. I have used exactly the same method to move people on, in the course of duty, and other dog-owners will find it useful in getting rid of undesirable callers at front or back door. (*See* p. 69 for the way to train a dog to do this.)

When patrolling on my own I often had to argue and, occasionally, even struggle with a criminal when trying to detain or arrest him; accompanied by a dog this was never necessary. If there were one, two, three or even four people to be taken to the police station they always came quietly, but I always made a point of getting the dog to play a part in detaining them. It helped in keeping them quiet, especially if they had had the experience of being 'found' or 'stopped' by the dog. In the early days a handler and his dog were reckoned to be worth a man and a half, but my opinion is that my dog was equal to any two men.

I remember one very miserable dark night, about twelve o'clock, when my thoughts were miles away and I was hurrying to go off duty, my dog suddenly 'pointed' into a large field overgrown with potato haulm and nettles some four feet high. Turning into the field, we had gone about 200 yards when suddenly we came on two men outstretched on the ground digging potatoes with their hands and putting them into a half-filled sack that lay between them. I don't know who was the more surprised as I shone my torch on them and said, 'Get up and have a go for it if you like, while the dog is in the mood.'

One of them replied, 'Not me, guv, I saw too much of that in Jerusalem.'

It was not a very important arrest perhaps, but it was certainly a credit to the dog, who had been concentrating on

her job more than I had. Later, at the police station, the two
men were identified as two who had been interviewed a week
earlier by a farmer and a C.I.D. officer. They were suspected
of stealing potatoes, but at that time, although the farmer was
sure the potatoes in their possession were his own King
Edwards, he could not prove it. My dog settled the issue
beyond all doubt.

By now I was in the happy position of being able to train
my colleagues with their dogs, including the author of *My Dog
Rex*, ex-P.C. Arthur Holman. The story of the activities of his
dog while in the police force is well told, but it has a very sad
ending.

In 1954 I retired from the police and began training dogs
on my own account, for that seemed the natural thing for me
to do. My previous activities in the police were known to many
and soon I had a clientele among people who wanted someone
to give their dogs obedience training. I set up my kennels on
the Metropolitan Water Board's ground at Hampton, where
I became established, and in course of time trained security
dogs and men handlers for the Metropolitan Water Board,
millionaire Paul Getty, Taylor-Woodrow, McAlpine, and the
local authorities at Wembley, Ealing, Ilford, West Ham,
Tottenham and Merton and Morden. I went out to Trinidad
with dogs for the Texaco Oil Company, and over the years I
have trained security dogs for many private people, including
women living in lonely places.

I also trained the dogs, and went to Rome, for the M.G.M
film *The Little Hut*, starring Ava Gardner, David Niven and
Stewart Granger. Believe me, directors of films are sometimes
very difficult people to please. They demand immediate
thought and action. It was my job to direct the dogs and to
make them do just what was asked of them. In one part of this
film the dog had to steal a fish. The dog did not like fish, but
I could not tell the director that, so I had to think fast. What I

did was to pour honey, which I knew the dog liked, into the
belly of the fish, slit open for that purpose. The opened belly of
the fish was placed farthest away from the camera, and the director
got his shot. Since then I have trained dogs for other films.

At the end of a course of training I always give a demonstration to owners of the dogs—other dogs, if qualified, also
taking part—followed by instructions to the owner on how
to carry on with the training from the point where I have left
off. One can never be quite sure how dogs, or even people,
will react after the training. I well remember a Mrs Flowers,
an American, coming to me with her miniature black poodle
Chou-Chou for a one-month training obedience course. It
was a lovely little dog, and responded very well indeed, and,
as usual, I invited Mrs Flowers to see the results, in Laleham
Park. She was accompanied by two other women, and remained
seated in a car some twenty yards away from where I was
giving the demonstration. When I had finished I waved to her
to come over to me to be re-introduced to her dog, a little
perturbed that all three ladies seemed to be sobbing into
handkerchiefs held up to their faces. Mrs Flowers in due time
came over to me, Chou-Chou recognising her immediately and
jumping round her. Mrs Flowers, however, was so overcome
with emotion that, still using her handkerchief to wipe away
her tears, she sank to the ground in front of me. Unable to
understand or cope with this unusual exhibition, I was speech-
less for a few moments, then, deciding I must do something to
end the embarrassment, I said, 'Please get up, Mrs Flowers, I
have some instructions to give you.'

After a little persuasion she eventually got to her feet and to
my surprise, in a rather choking voice, said, 'Oh, Mr Scott,
Mr Scott, I am in ecstasy with happiness.'

This led to my having her other miniature poodle, named
Mon-Cher, to train, as well as a toy poodle called Impi, owned
by one of the other women in the car. I am not easily sur-

prised, but Impi certainly astonished me when, on the first occasion that I saw her at her home, a tin of beer was poured into a basin for her and she drank the lot. She only just had time to climb on to a settee before she fell asleep. It was a daily occurrence, I was told.

My success with these dogs led to a number of poodles coming to me for training, all from Americans attached to the same base as Mrs Flowers.

I include this story as it illustrates the rewarding efforts I experience in training other people's dogs in 'obedience', and it emphasises that dogs trained by a professional can give immense satisfaction to owners who may have doubts about having his or her dog trained by a professional.

Occasionally I have the pleasure of being asked to go to private houses to train dogs. One such was at Trewoon, St Austell, my Cornwall 'seat', where dwell two St Bernards, Bruno and Sultan, noble creatures indeed.

I find most breeds of dogs easy to train in obedience, particularly Alsatians, Labradors, all the collies, Shetlands especially, poodles and dachshunds. There are, however, some 5 per cent that are quite hopeless. They seem to be either sick or demented, and they represent my failures. Forty per cent are sent to me as a last resort, which is quite understandable, but the rest I find a pleasure to train.

I might mention that many pleasant social activities come my way as a result of services rendered in training dogs. Recently the Scotch of St James's (London SW1) were kind enough to make me a life member of their club.

In this book I have purposely arranged each exercise in obedience and security training under separate headings so that a particular exercise can be referred to easily and quickly, and I have written the text as simply as possible without delving into a great deal of detail regarding the psychology of dogs. Much has already been written on this latter subject, and

B

although the information may appeal to theorists and others, it is not easily understood by the average dog-owner and is not always necessary for those people who merely want to train their own dogs. I believe the instructions given in the following pages will be of practical use to the majority of dog-owners who wish their dogs to be well-behaved and useful companions, and all the obedience lessons can be used to instil basic training in any dog in the kindest possible way.

I have trained many dogs for ordinary people who had not the slightest idea how to go about it, but I would like to make it clear that to handle or train any dog, including those required for security purposes, does not require prior experience. All that is needed is adequate information on the subject, such as will be found in this book, and a liberal amount of common sense. Dogs trained for security patrol work in public places would not be tolerated in Britain if they were used as lethal weapons. The appellation 'guard dog' is often associated with security patrol dog, but the two types are quite different. The training of the guard dog is as nothing compared with the security patrol dog, which is trained with a handler and, by virtue of that fact, acts only on the commands of that handler. All that is required of the guard dog is that he should have an uncertain temperament and be of an unfriendly nature. It is generally left on its own in an enclosed place to frighten people off, it has no one to look after its welfare or give it orders during the period it is on duty, and all that it can achieve is a moral effect in protecting that property. The so-called guard may be a cheap proposition in the beginning, but it can prove expensive if there is an aftermath of complaints. The guard dog is, generally, a baited dog, and may become a lethal weapon; it is, as a rule, given very little training, if any, and is often the subject of much adverse criticism in the national press, thereby sometimes bringing the Alsatian and other breeds into disrepute.

The intention of this book is that it should be regarded as an instructional manual rather than a book to be read. Obedience is essential in the security patrol dog, and although I have separated the sections on 'Obedience' and 'Security Training' the two are complementary and should be studied together. The book is also intended to be useful for practical purposes rather than competitive training, although several people have reaped rewards in police dog trials by following the instructions laid down, and I trust others will benefit likewise.

I would like to express my gratitude to the dog handlers of the Metropolitan Water Board for their ready assistance, to the photographer, who wishes to remain anonymous, in memory to his dog Bruce, and in particular to Mr S. Whittingham Boothe for his kindly and patient assistance in editing this work.

T.S.

Introduction

While, throughout, this book is primarily intended for those who wish to train a dog for security work, and the instructions are based on knowledge obtained in training dogs for criminal work by police and civilian handlers, the obedience exercises have much wider application. Animals cannot be trained to do anything useful until they have learnt to obey commands; indeed, they are often nuisances until they have learnt to be obedient. The pity is that many dog-owners are content so long as their pets don't disgrace themselves in the home or in someone else's house, yet house training, important though it is, is unimportant if that same animal is the cause of an accident leading to permanent disability in a human being, or even death. Most of the road accidents caused by dogs could have been avoided if the animal involved had been taught obedience, hence every dog-owner owes it to himself, his dog, and the general public to see that the animal he owns and is responsible for knows how to behave not only in the home but also in public places, particularly on the highway. Obedience training is quite simple to teach, but it calls for patience and determination, both of which are rewarded by a deeper affection and understanding springing up between the trainer and the animal being trained. It can be fun for both.

Relationships Between Dog and Trainer
Before beginning to train any dog there should be a clear

mental picture in the mind of the trainer of what he intends to teach the dog and of what the dog's reactions are likely to be. The words chosen as words of command, and the appropriate signals given with them, play a most important part. It should be borne in mind that the number of commands a dog can understand and retain will be few, and that no two people speak in exactly the same way. The words chosen should be monosyllabic and easy to remember. A standard pattern should be followed so that if a dog has to be transferred to another handler for some reason, although the animal will have to get used to a new voice and practically have to learn a new language, at least the words will not be entirely unfamiliar. Commands should be given in a well-articulated manner, and signals distinctive, particularly in obedience training.

In security training care must be given to the choice of commands so that they do not confuse with other words that might at some time give offence. This is of special importance if an appearance in the police court may be necessary, since the expressions used by a handler might influence a magistrate. For instance, directions to a dog to 'Seize him', 'Do him', or even 'Get him' are frowned on. In evidence, 'Stop him' will cause no offence if the handler has been called on to describe his actions and instructions to his dog. Again, a person who is being charged might say you told the dog to 'Attack him' when you actually said 'At him'. I well remember explaining to a magistrate that the name of a dog I had at the time was Caesar, and that I had not directed my dog to 'seize' the prisoner.

Progress with any dog will depend entirely on the handler. He should never try to train a dog when he is tired or not feeling up to scratch because he will need every bit of concentration he can muster for his dog. A good keen dog reflects his handler's ability.

A dog usually takes to a handler after a few days. This is a point worth noting when selecting a dog. I have found that during the trial period a dog automatically forms an attachment for his handler and will seldom go far out of sight, even when allowed to go on his own, the line being attached, of course, just in case the dog might take it into its head to bolt off. At the same time it must be appreciated that a good deal depends on how the handler gains the affection of his dog. He should be firm without in any way being cruel, and always patient and understanding, correcting the animal only when necessary, and then only when the dog is doing something he should not be doing. The correction must be made always at the time of wrongdoing, not afterwards. A good handler will turn to advantage any failings the dog reveals during training. For instance, if the dog attempts to follow his handler after being left in the 'down' position, noting the dog's action the handler will immediately point to the place he wants the dog to 'Go back' to, using that expression in a stern voice, and eventually using the word 'Go' as the word of command to make the dog go in any direction he requires. The motion of the hand used at the same time becomes the signal for that command.

Equipment

For training a dog, in addition to a leather collar and lead, the following will be required. (*See* pp. 116, 117.)

A twelve-yard rope line with a swivel at the end similar to that on the end of his lead.

An iron pin about two feet long by half an inch in diameter, with a curved loop at one end, and a point at the other, so that it can be pushed into the ground without too much effort.

All the dog's food in a tin (one and a half pounds of raw meat, preferably shin or cheek of bullock and mutton breast), cut into small pieces about the size of an Oxo cube.

A cloth bag, about twelve inches by twelve inches, with a sling attached that can be wound round the neck of the bag to prevent anything falling out. The bag will be easy for the dog to carry, and it will hold all the working tools.

The dog should always wear a leather collar, a choke, chain collar being used only during the early stages of obedience training. When the choke, chain collar is used it must be put on correctly. The pull on the chain should come across the head of the dog, not from the ground, when the dog is in the heeling position. If it is put on the wrong way it will shave the hair from the dog's neck. Never use a chain collar in any training that requires the dog to do something on its own. This applies to teaching a dog to retrieve and carry when on the lead; a jerk may put the dog 'off'. In any case, try to dispense with this type of collar as early as possible. It should never be left on a dog, or be used to tie him up when kennelling or for other reasons because it is possible for the dog to strangle himself if the chain collar gets caught up on something. If used permanently it may shave off all the hair on its neck, and it tends to give the animal a 'hard neck' which makes him insensitive to the commands the handler has been trying to teach him. This type of collar may look imposing but it can be lethal, and if it should prove fatal to the dog the handler will have only himself to blame.

As most of the dog's work will be done in the open, begin his training under such conditions. Keep to a schedule by practising each exercise at the same time of the day each day. The morning is the best time, and it is wiser to choose a different location each day if possible.

Selecting a Dog for Security Work
The need for dogs with handlers trained in security work is becoming more evident and necessary every day, so much so that the supply cannot always keep up with the demand.

Wherever dog patrols have been employed crime has become less, and sometimes stopped altogether, particularly so when employed by local authorities and factories and on estates. Many householders, after having been burgled, have had their dogs trained for protection purposes in the home or to guard cars when they have to leave them unattended.

Several breeds of dogs may be used for security work, among them the Labrador, Airedale Terrier and Boxer. The Alsatian, however, as has been proved, can surpass them all, being the most used, the most abused and hated, and the best-loved of any breed, particularly so because 50 per cent of the value of the dog lies in its moral effect, which is the reason all the services have chosen the Alsatian.

Only about one Alsatian in ten has the qualifications for making a good police or security dog. (Throughout, when I use the term 'dog' it also includes the bitch of the species, unless specifically stated otherwise.) This is because of the very wide range of temperaments to be found in this breed, as will be understood if one thinks of the number employed by the Blind Association, where the reasons for choosing a dog for this type of work are the exact opposite to those required for a dog employed in security work.

Because of the wide range of temperaments in dogs it is sometimes necessary to try out several dogs before finding one that meets the needs, and they should be on trial for about two weeks to ascertain whether they have the necessary qualifications. The dog chosen for security work should be of average height, of standard proportions, any colour but white, bold but not ferocious, and about twelve months old. Take particular notice that the dog is not a monorchid; in fact, be certain that it isn't, because monorchids are very temperamental. A dog that is hand-shy, runs behind its kennel when approached or suffers from hip displacement is seldom worth training. Of course, there will be other factors in the make-up of a dog that will influence selection. Dropped ears, for example, make an Alsatian look sloppy and spoil its alert appearance. They are not, however, detrimental to the working abilities of the animal—I have trained many with good results —but it loses them favour. Again, long-haired Alsatians are frowned on in England, chiefly because this condition is considered a fault in the breed and is a handicap to them in the show ring. They are used extensively in Europe, especially on the borders of Germany, to combat smuggling, mainly because they can stand up to bad climatic conditions better than short-haired Alsatians. They are naturally less favoured in hot climates. Long-haired Alsatians are said to be bred once in every fourth generation, therefore we should be chary of condemning what Nature herself produces. Personally I have always found their working qualifications excellent.

For security work, before any obedience training is given to a dog on trial, ascertain whether or not the animal will hold on to a sack or similar material. The object of this is easily understood when it is realised that the sack, later, will be wrapped round the arm for training in 'man work'. If after a week the animal refuses to hold on to a sack, then that dog is no good for security work and should be returned to its owner.

To discover whether the dog will hold on to a sack, tie the dog on the lead to a wall or fence. It will be noted that the dog so tied can move only in a half-circle, so that, if the dog *will* work on a sack, the handler is in a safe position to estimate the movement of the dog. The handler thus avoids being bitten and the dog is obliged automatically to face him.

It is particularly important that the dog is fitted with a leather collar so that it cannot injure itself or be put off 'holding' by a sudden jerk on its neck, which will certainly happen if it is fitted with a choke, chain collar. (*See* pp. 116 and 117 for information about leads and collars.)

Wave a sack or cloth in front of the dog, and let him hold

on to it if possible. This may have to be done a few times to begin with to encourage him. Let him hold and pull the sack from you. Then let him jump for the sack and pull it. Sometimes it may be necessary to threaten him with a thin stick, held in the free hand, but on no account hurt the animal or hit its face; strike the ground several times and let the whole exercise seem to be in the nature of a game. At the same time that the sack is flicked in front of the dog say 'Stop him', so that the animal associates this action with the word of command. Repeat the command several times. Very few dogs will hold on to a sack, but it is essential that the security or police dog should do so. Only that type of dog will train for the kind of work required. The person appointed to be the handler should be the only one to say 'Stop him', and the only one to praise the dog and pat him, which should be done immediately the dog has held on or attempts to hold on to the sack. Then let some other person shake the sack in front of the dog. He may have to flick it so that the end of the sack enters the dog's mouth. In this part of the exercise the handler should be standing behind the dog, encouraging him to hold on. The assistant may have to use the thin stick and threaten to use it, in the same way as the handler did earlier, if the dog does not go for the sack.

As soon as the handler is satisfied that the dog will hold on to a sack at this stage, he should take the lead in both hands and ask the assistant to shake the sack in front of the dog, and this time to step backwards a few paces, then again and again, faster and faster until he is trotting backwards, still waving the sack. Practise this for about fifteen minutes three times a day, and if the dog follows up and pulls the sack, be satisfied that that dog will make good.

Another method of making a dog hold on to a sack is by placing a walking stick or a piece of wood of similar size inside the sack, and wrapping the sack round the stick, then inducing the dog to hold the sack. If necessary, the dog's legs should be gently tapped with this contraption. Of course, if the dog makes any attempt to hold on, then remove the stick and proceed as already stated.

When you feel quite sure the dog is capable of holding on, take him to a veterinary surgeon and have him examined to ascertain if he is physically fit for security work. This is essential and should never be omitted because a considerable amount of time and expense will be involved in the training of the dog. A certificate of inoculation should also be available; otherwise insist on the dog being re-inoculated. The vet's examination being satisfactory, training the dog can begin. Obedience and security training are taught together during the period of the eight-week course.

Always insist on being given the pedigree with the dog. It is never possible to tell how good a dog will turn out to be, and if it should be an exceptionally good dog, it may be profitable to breed from him.

Mongrels are generally a doubtful proposition, and if they were better than pure-bred dogs then there would be no pure-bred dogs. Mongrels, as a rule, inherit the faults of both parents. Nevertheless, bear in mind that pedigree and performance are two different things.

A Note on Monorchids

I have had many monorchids for obedience training—I find they average about one in eight of Alsatian dogs—but I would not like to work with one, which is how I assess a dog's worth. A question I always ask myself when I select a dog is: 'Would I be willing to work with that dog?' And if it is a monorchid the answer is 'No'. Anyone who has worked with a monorchid will, I believe, be of the same opinion as myself.

It may not be generally known, but more often than not

monorchids in middle life have to be operated on for removal of the testicle that has failed to descend, because it has become malignant. The operation, incidentally, costs about ten guineas, a point which must have some influence on selection. No such dog is allowed in any show ring or test sponsored by the Kennel Club, which could be disheartening to a handler. I would not like to give the impression that I believe all monorchids or cryptorchids should be condemned out of hand, for no doubt some are faithful companions to their owners, nevertheless I would not advocate selecting them for security work.

I

Obedience Training

'HAND'

This is the word of command to call a dog to hand or to come to its owner or handler.

This exercise is divided into two stages and, for simplicity in arranging the book, both stages are described here. The second stage, however, cannot be satisfactorily taught until the dog has learnt the meaning of the command 'Down' (*see* p. 34) and, therefore, it should not be attempted until then. If this seems a little confusing to the reader he should try to realise that if, as a dog-owner, he tries to combine exercises and teach his dog more than one simple lesson at a time he will end up with a totally confused dog and, unfairly, set the dog down as a nitwit incapable of learning.

Stage 1

Put the choke, chain collar on the dog's neck, for the initial training of this exercise, then attach the leather lead, which should be at least four feet long; anything shorter will soon prove of little use.

Have the tin containing small pieces of meat close at hand or, better still, have several pieces of meat in a convenient pocket, and stand the length of the lead away from the dog. The position of the dog will not matter so long as he is facing you.

Have the lead in your left hand and a piece of meat in your right hand and gently pull the dog towards you, at the same time saying the dog's name, 'Pooch', or whatever it is, and calling with the word of command, 'Hand'. It does not matter whether you use this particular word of command to call the dog, but it *does* matter that you use the same word of command every time you want the dog to come to you. A dog is very much a creature of habit, and the same command and signal should always be used every time you require your dog to act in a certain way.

At the same time as the command for the dog to come to hand is given, place the right hand low down in front of the right hip, with the meat exposed to view in the right hand so that it can easily be seen by the dog. The motion of the right hand holding the meat should always be combined as a signal reinforcing the command every time the dog is called to hand.

Have the meat in the palm of the hand when the animal takes it. If held in the fingers, as likely as not he will bite the fingers in his eagerness to get the meat quickly. He should be rewarded immediately each time he obeys the command, praised, patted and encouraged as much as possible with such words as 'Good boy'. Try to get him to understand that coming to hand is the one thing in his life that he most wants to do. He *will* enjoy doing it, and it should be his greatest pleasure.

When the handler is sure the dog understands this command while on the lead, practise on the twelve-yard line so that the dog can be taught to come from a distance. Every time he hesitates, give the line a jerk with sufficient force to make him obey; even draw him forward if necessary.

Do these exercises several times each day until the dog understands that at the command 'Hand', or the signal for that command, he must come to you without hesitation. As he

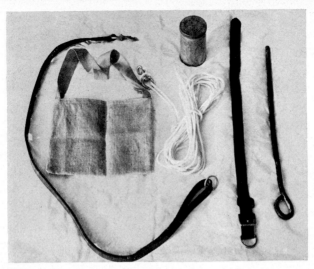

Equipment: leather lead about 4 feet long and 1¼ inch wide with running ring in the loop; cloth bag about 12 inches square to carry the equipment; tin to carry 1½ lb of meat cut in small pieces; rope line about 12 yards long with trigger catch attached; leather collar 1¼ inches wide by 26 inches long with D ring at the end for extra strength; iron pin about 2 feet long with a loop at one end.

'Hand'. Stand about five yards from the dog, with rope line attached. Draw the dog gently towards you with left hand, having a piece of meat in the right to give to the dog when he comes. Then stand at greater distances and repeat, saying 'Hand' on each occasion.

'*Sit*'. Draw the line tight in the left hand and jerk upwards, using both hands to give the command. Later use only the right hand as the signal, giving the command 'sit' on each occasion.

From the front 'sit' position, induce the dog with meat to follow your hand round behind you; then let him have the meat when he sits on your left.

progresses in learning to obey, his reward can be reduced, first to every other time he obeys, and eventually to only occasionally.

Stage 2

As explained above, completion of the exercise on coming to hand is best left until the dog has learned to go 'down'.

The dog will be at one end of the long line, the other end of which is tied to an iron pin pushed into the ground as far as it will go. Make sure the pin cannot be pulled out by a sudden jerk if the dog should suddenly decide to bolt off. Call the dog to hand, reward him, and put him in the down position. Then call him from different directions, and every time he obeys reward him and again place him in the down position. Don't forget that the dog's ability to come to you is limited by the length of the line. Always take care that he does not get a jolt on his neck because you have accidentally stood on the line or because, having called him from too great a distance, he is jerked to a stop as the line becomes taut. Repeat the exercise until you are satisfied he knows what you want him to do.

Next, take the line off the pin, hold the end of the line yourself, allow the dog to run about you, and then call him to hand. If you feel sure the dog is going to respond, allow him to run freely with the line still attached to the collar, call him, and reward and praise him as before. Should the dog not come to you when you wish him to, but tends to hesitate when you are not holding the line, it should not be difficult for you to put your foot out and tread on the line, and draw the animal back to you. Call the dog, on each occasion, just as he is getting towards the end of the line.

Practise this under all sorts of conditions, especially when you are taking him for quiet walks. Hide behind trees or other cover, call the dog at short intervals to start with, then allow a longer time to elapse before calling him and very soon

C

you will notice that he will hardly ever let you out of his sight.

The dog must always obey. First do the exercises without anyone else being present, then with people about. It is essential that you only reward the dog when he comes to you. If he refuses to come to you for his meat-reward, starve him for a day or so. This will probably happen to begin with, but don't worry, he will soon understand what is required.

When a dog is hesitant in coming to hand during the above exercises it is advisable to keep him on the lead or line for a month or more when he is taken out for exercise. Feed him only one piece of meat at a time, and then only when he obeys the command, 'Hand'. Let him receive *all* his food for this exercise only and, if necessary, cut him down to half-rations.

Do not get the idea that a dog needs to be off the lead in order to be properly exercised. I could not afford to allow any dog to run free unless I was absolutely sure that he could be trusted to return to me when I called to him. All dogs entrusted to me are always on the line or lead while they are with me during my four-week course. They are given plenty of walking to keep them fit. They are not my dogs, and I would be wasting valuable time in trying to get them back if they ran off, apart from risking my reputation if they were irretrievably lost.

Command by Whistle

The method of training a dog to a whistle is the same as for calling a dog to hand. Instead of saying 'Hand', the whistle is blown, and the dog rewarded if he obeys. The dog should, of course, be taught to come to hand verbally, together with the hand signal, before the whistle method is introduced. Then, in the initial stages of using a whistle, both the verbal command and the whistle should be given together. In other words, say 'Hand', then immediately blow the whistle. After a little while the whistle only need be used. To make the dog go down with the whistle, substitute 'Down' for 'Hand', but the appropriate note on the whistle (*see* below) must be used and it must be accompanied by the hand signal to go 'down'.

A silent whistle may be used to call a dog to hand or to go down; indeed this type of whistle is well worth having and is of great practical use if the dog is trained to respond from a distance. Such whistles can be adjusted to suit any particular dog, and a dog's hearing is well adapted to respond to them. However, the signals given on any whistle are very limited. The only practical variations are a series of short blasts for the dog to come to hand, and one long one for the dog to go down.

'SIT'
This is the word of command given when the handler wishes his dog to sit.

This lesson is best carried out when the handler is walking with the dog at his left side. After walking about six paces, stop quickly, jerk the lead upwards with the left hand and, at the same time, say 'Sit'. Repeat this several times, jerking the lead upwards every time you stop, until the dog sits without its being necessary to jerk the lead at all.

With some dogs it may be expedient to jerk the lead upwards with the *right* hand and at the same time to press downwards on the dog's back with the left hand, but do try to use only the lead if possible.

After a day or so, when you feel that the dog understands this exercise so far, walk with him quickly, stop, and encourage him to sit without your having to jerk the lead. Repeat this until eventually he sits automatically every time you stop.

Every now and again one comes across a dog that will not sit, even when the lead is jerked upwards or pressure is put on his back. The remedy is, instead of jerking the lead, to lift the dog's front feet two or three inches above the ground by drawing the lead upwards with both hands. The weight of the dog will then fall on both back legs, and of necessity the dog must sit. Let the front legs then gently come to rest on the ground, and make the dog stay in the sit position for several minutes.

This exercise takes about a week to perfect, depending, of course, on the dog and the ability of the handler. Practise on your left and right sides. (*See* 'Right', p. 33.)

Try to insist that the dog sits close to the knee when you stop walking forward, and that he faces the direction in which you are going. It may be necessary, especially in the early stages of making a dog sit by one's side, to bend down and draw him towards that knee with the hand, saying to the dog, 'Closer'. A dog that is merely taught to sit on command may adopt a slovenly habit and sit facing in any direction, if not corrected at the beginning of the exercise. Also, once you yourself have stopped, do not move your feet to oblige the dog in your attempt to make him sit in the proper manner. Nothing looks worse than a handler moving in all directions to try to make his dog obey him.

Later, when the dog sits automatically whenever you stop (after 'heeling' on your left side), take a pace to your right and draw the dog by the lead to your left knee, saying 'Closer'. Repeat this several times and insist that the dog sits correctly on every occasion. You may have to jerk the lead in the initial stages in order to get results, but the actions will instil in the dog the necessity of sitting as close as possible to his handler.

The same kind of procedure must also be applied when you call a dog to hand and want him to sit. Make the dog sit in front of you, by drawing him to you when you say 'Hand', and when he is quite close up to you, with his nose almost touching you, jerk the lead upwards with the left hand. Forefingers of both hands should be in the same position, pointing towards the dog and parallel with the ground. Reward the dog from the right hand. When he understands the word 'Sit' use the right forefinger only as the sign to sit, the use of the lead in the left hand gradually being dispensed with.

'SPEAK'

This is the word of command to a dog when the handler wishes him to bark. For security dogs it is incorporated with the command 'Watch him' (see p. 68).

To teach a dog to speak on command first tie him to a wall or fence, using leather collar and lead only. He should be able to move in a half-circle as described under 'Selecting a Dog for Security Work' (p. 16). Approach the dog with a very thin stick in the right hand and a piece of meat in the left. Say 'Speak', loudly, and raise the right hand as though you intend to strike him. Should he bark or give tongue, reward him immediately.

If you meet with success as early as this, then continue to make him speak frequently, using the command every time. Follow this routine for several days until you know he will speak on command every time he is directed to do so either by you or any other person.

The next step is to use the right hand only, with the same upward motion as was used with the stick, and then, as soon as you can, omit the use of the right hand and use only the word of command, 'Speak'. The final aim of this stage is to get the dog to speak when the hand is raised and no verbal command is given, but also when no hand movement accompanies the verbal command. The reason for getting the dog to learn both alternatives is fairly obvious but will be quite clear before the end of this lesson.

If the dog is slow in barking, attempt to hit him or strike the ground beside him. If there is still no response you will have to hit him with the stick, on the front legs only, gently at first, then harder if he will not speak. Every time the right hand is raised, whether holding a stick or not, say the word 'Speak'. This should be given loudly in the initial stages, but as the dog makes progress the voice should be moderated until eventually it becomes a whisper.

Although the stick will eventually be dispensed with, the motion of raising the right hand from the centre of the body upwards as far as it will go should always be used when the dog is required to speak. The exercise should be practised several times a day, particularly when the dog comes to hand and sits in front of you. Note this last phrase, which indicates the continuity of the training, the joining of one phase of learning on to the next. Teaching a dog to speak may take some time, but the average dog answers perfectly in about a week.

The reason for teaching a dog to speak by raising the hand, with or without a stick, will be readily understood when it is realised that if a wrongdoer is disturbed while being sought for, almost invariably he will take up exactly the same attitude to try to make the dog go away from him. If the dog has been taught to speak by this method he will automatically bark all the louder, thus informing the handler where his dog and the wrongdoer are.

If there is difficulty in getting a dog to speak by the foregoing methods, as is possible with very shy animals, another way is to tie him to fence or wall, as explained earlier, and to walk off as though you were going to leave him. (You will have to do part of the walking away backwards.) Every few paces, call to the dog 'Speak', and at the same time raise the stick held in the right hand. You may have to go about fifty yards before the dog attempts to speak, but as soon as it does, run back immediately and reward and praise him lavishly. Repeat this until you have got him speaking well. Then revert to the stages previously described.

The dog that is to be trained in security work, after he has learned to speak on command immediately and without hesitation, should now be taught to bark, with the command, 'Watch him' added. This sounds more appropriate when approaching crowds of people who have to be dispersed. As stated, the new command is simply an additional one tacked on to 'Speak', which is eventually dropped. (For further explanation *see* under 'Stop him', p. 68.)

Have several people stand in a line in front of the dog and get each, in turn, to make the dog speak. This is to get the dog to understand that you want him to bark at anybody. This is most important in security work because the dog, later, must speak every time he finds a person hiding away or at the end of a 'track', especially at night-time when he is acting as the eyes and ears of the handler. Unless the dog speaks readily when he finds a person it is impossible for the handler to know where dog or quarry is in the dark, since the dog will be off the lead, possibly searching premises, and some distance away.

The dog should be encouraged to give tongue at anything unusual he may notice during exercise and when at work, and be praised lavishly on each occasion. Even in the home, if a dog gives tongue during his period of rest, especially at night, the reason for his barking should be investigated, and he should never be suppressed by telling him to be quiet. A dog generally accedes to his master's wishes, and learns accordingly. Therefore, if he is continually directed to keep quiet when at home and something unusual is occurring, the time may come when an intruder is about and the dog will take no notice. The handler must, of course, be guided by common sense and not allow the dog to become a nuisance.

I well remember more than one occasion when I was called

to premises where there were believed to be suspects and from which a criminal had left hurriedly. Taken with me to the scene by car, my police dog Chum, after picking up a track, would lead me through the back gardens of many houses, from the back windows of which I have seen dogs of all breeds gazing at us without attempting to give tongue. All these dogs had been suppressed by their owners from barking warning of intruders, whereas if they had been encouraged to do so no intruder would have ventured near the premises.

The instructions that will be found under the command 'Seek' (p. 78) will help to instil into a dog the art of giving tongue at anything unusual, and at the end of the exercise on 'Stop him' (p. 68) there will be found instructions for teaching the dog crowd work.

'HEEL'

This is the command when the handler wishes his dog to take up position by his heel on the left-hand side and in the direction in which the handler is facing.

Getting a dog to 'heel' is a little more difficult for the dog than the previous three lessons since he is expected to perform more than one simple action. This means that the handler is called on to use more concentration and display a little more dexterity to assist the dog to perform what, to him, will seem a complicated manœuvre.

Slip the choke, chain collar on the dog for the initial stages of this lesson. The word of command is 'Heel', and by that you mean that the dog is to come to heel on your *left* side. In some schools, and in show work, when the dog has been brought into a sitting position facing the handler, on the command 'Recover' the dog comes up to heel by going round the right of the handler and behind him. I see no point at all in trying to add another word to his vocabulary. 'Recover' means the same thing to him as 'heel' does, and that is, come to heel on the left side. When he has learnt to obey that command, although he will not be aware of it, he will also have learnt which is your left side, but by a different name. In the next lesson, 'Right', he will find out which is your right side, and he will know it by that name. For myself, I do not want a dog to heel anywhere else than on my left or right side, therefore a third word is an unnecessary addition to the dog's vocabulary.

Begin with the dog in the sit position, facing you, with the lead in your right hand. Give the command 'Heel', draw him towards your right side and, with as continuous a movement as possible, pull him round the back of you to your left-hand side, and make him sit there. This is comparatively easy, but the action is facilitated if you have a piece of meat in the right hand and transfer it to your left as the dog is passing behind you. (If you find this difficult, then have a piece of meat in both hands.) It will probably be necessary to do this several times before the dog gets the right idea, but it is rather like a game to him, and with perseverence you should get results after a few days of practice. Reward the dog when he completes the heel and is sitting correctly on your left. (It is most important that the dog sits correctly, as described earlier, on p. 26).

Before proceeding further it is as well to mention here that when you are about to walk off and to give the command 'Heel', make sure you are holding the lead correctly. Both hands should be on the lead as though you were about to play the piano, that is, with the palms of the hands downwards. I emphasise this and hope that the use of the word 'piano' will help it to register, because an untrained dog may pull you round, and if your hand is already half twisted it could be injured if the dog is suddenly attracted by a cat or other animal and decides to give chase. For that reason, *do* hold the lead correctly with left hand on the lead, and near the collar to guide the dog if necessary. There is no need to hold the lead with the left hand all the time as, in turning right about, it will often be found advantageous to use the left *leg* as a fulcrum for the lead. The left hand can thus be used to pat the leg to encourage the dog to turn right.

Place the right hand in the loop of the lead, or twist the lead round the right hand if it is necessary to shorten it for convenience. The right hand is the anchor hand.

The command 'Heel' can be more deeply impressed on the dog by making him sit on your left and starting to walk with him on the word 'Heel'. Stop after several paces and jerk the lead upwards with the left hand, at the same time give the command 'Sit', continue walking forward with the command 'Heel', then stop and order the dog to sit again. Practise several times for a few days until the dog understands 'Heel' perfectly. Vary the direction by walking in the form of a large figure 8, and make turns in many directions, stopping at intervals of about six paces. Whenever the dog is walking by your left side insist that he heels properly and does not give others the impression that he is taking *you* for a walk by pulling on the lead some distance ahead of you. If after a few paces the dog goes forward too much or pulls on the lead, then, with both hands on the lead, jerk the dog backwards so that he is lifted off the ground and pulled back sharply as far behind you as he was in front of you, but take care that he lands on his feet. Continue walking forwards and repeat as is necessary until the dog understands that he must walk to heel correctly. With the average dog it is not generally necessary to jerk him to order more than three times if you have done this as it should be done.

Later, vary the speed you walk, and run occasionally so that the dog learns to proceed at the pace you want to travel.

To perfect walking to heel, approach several posts one at a time, and as you get near each post walk to the right of it. If the dog goes to the left, as will probably happen to start with, give him an extra pull *at the same time* that the post stops him, and draw him back to your left knee. He will soon understand, after he has hit against three or four posts, to pass them on the right and to keep close to heel on your left side of any obstacle. There may come a time when you may have to run past an obstacle to get somewhere quickly, with the dog on the lead, and if the dog hasn't learnt this lesson you may both come an awful cropper.

'RIGHT'
This is the order given to a dog when you wish him to come to heel at your right side.

After having learnt to come up on your left-hand side, the dog is next taught to come up on your right-hand side. It is necessary that he should learn to walk on both sides because, if you are accompanied by someone who is on one side of you, you will want the dog on the opposite side, or you may be walking on a narrow footpath where it is to the advantage of both dog and handler that the animal is on the inside should the handler wish to step off the kerb; if the dog is on the outside, in stepping off the kerb he may tread on the dog.

'Heel', therefore, means heel on the left, and 'Right' means heel on the right.

For this lesson, start with the dog sitting on the left side. On the command 'Right', your actions will be the reverse of those used for 'Heel'. That is, the lead and meat will be transferred to the right hand and the dog drawn behind you to your right. Make the dog sit after each 'Heel' and 'Right' command, and be sure to reward him each time he obeys the command successfully. Don't expect the dog to 'Right' when he is sitting in front of you; he must previously have been on the left and in the heel position.

Once you have got him to perform the transposition from

left- to right-hand side successfully, practise, when walking, getting him to transfer from left to right on the command 'Right' and back again to the left on the command 'Heel'. By this time he will need no reward for obeying orders.

'DOWN'

This is the command to the dog when you want him to lie down with his forepaws in front of him and his hind legs tucked under him. It is similar to the 'sit' position but his forequarters will be down as well as his rear.

When you direct a dog to lie down, *never* prefix the command with 'Sit'. If you do, the dog will surely get confused. Say 'Down' only.

To make a dog go down, stand in front of him, the lead in the left hand extended as far as it will go from the left shoulder. Then, with the palm of the right hand strike the lead in the middle as hard as you can, and at the same time say 'Down'. In striking the lead, the right hand should start as far as possible above the handler's head, descend vertically on the lead, and continue in its movement until it almost touches his right knee-cap.

It does not matter if the animal is standing or sitting when you do this, but the harder you strike the lead the better will the dog understand the command, which must be obeyed immediately on all occasions. This is particularly important in security training when the order embodies with it a direction for the dog to let go of a criminal's arm. If the dog yelps when the lead is struck with the right hand, so much the better, since its effect will make a deeper impression on him if he is some distance away, and he will react immediately.

The action of the right hand on the lead when making the dog go down should now be adopted as the signal for him to do so. The command and signal, apart from security work, can be the means of saving a dog's life if he should be free and about, say, to cross a road, and you are able to anticipate danger. Practise the lesson several times a day, and the dog will quickly learn to understand what is required of him.

If you feel confident the dog understands this lesson so far, then use the line instead of the lead, as described under the second stage of training to heel. Tie one end of the line to the dog's collar, and the other to the iron pin pushed hard into the ground. Place the dog in the down position, near the pin, and stand twice the distance of the line away from dog and pin. Call the dog. Anticipate the moment when the dog is about to reach the end of the line, and say 'Down'. At the same time give the signal for that command and take a step towards the dog as you give signal and command. The dog will be jolted by the line on his neck, and it is most important that the jerk on the neck, signal, and command coincide so that they impress on him that he must go down immediately when ordered. Now go back to the pin, call the dog to hand, make him sit, and reward him. Do this exercise a number of times, rewarding the dog only when you have called him to hand and are back standing beside the pin with the dog in the sit position beside you. Never, *never* praise the dog when he has gone down. If you do, he will surely get up. He must stay in the down position until directed otherwise.

The often-used method of placing the left hand on the dog's back and pressing it down, at the same time drawing his head down with the lead in the right hand, has very little practical value. If you are some distance away or the dog is free it is impossible to convey any kind of signal to the dog, who will be unable to understand what you want him to do. Also, trying to drag the dog's head down with the right hand generally ends up by one hurting one's fingers on the ground. If an opportunity presents itself for you to observe a farmer or shepherd directing his dog to go down, you will never see him rap his fingers on the ground.

Sometimes, with dogs that are on the keen side or difficult to handle, it may be necessary to place the left foot on the lead and draw the lead under the hollow of the instep, with both hands on the lead. If you have to do this, do it quickly before the dog understands what you are up to, otherwise he may retaliate. As a precaution wear Wellingtons, then, if the dog snaps, he will only bite the Wellingtons. Keep the dog down for about a minute. Next time, pull the lead going under the foot with the left hand only, and make the down signal with the right hand as described at the beginning of this exercise. With very difficult dogs use a muzzle, particularly heavy dogs and those of large size. Dogs so treated soon understand that they must submit quickly.

To use a whistle with this exercise, *see* 'Hand', p. 24.

'STAY'

This is the command to the dog when you wish him to remain where he has been put.

Start with the dog in the down position, with the leather lead attached to the collar. Put the iron pin through the loop of the lead, or iron ring on the lead, then drive it into the ground. The pin must be firmly fixed. Walk round the dog saying 'Down', followed by 'Stay', and keep repeating the command 'Down' if he attempts to get up. Walk *over* the dog several times. When you walk round him, the distance between you and the dog should gradually be increased, but not to more than twenty yards during the first week. The object of the exercise is to make the dog understand that he must stay in the down position no matter how far you are away from him, therefore if the dog attempts to get up or gets up as you increase your distance from him you are wasting your time if you increase that distance before being sure that he will stay down. Continue saying 'Down' and 'Stay' and step over the dog a number of times. Occasionally, run past him.

Swing the rope line, folded into suitable lengths, round the dog or use another lead as you step over and walk round him. (Use the line or lead in the right hand and walk round the dog in an anti-clockwise direction so that you are between lead and dog and not likely accidentally to hit him.) Also, use an old metal drum, pail or anything that will make a noise, and beat it with a stick over the dog so that he will get used to all kinds of noises. Then throw the drum, pail or whatever it is in front of the dog, then over him. When first swinging the lead or line and using the drum or pail start gently and take great care to see that anything swung or thrown over the dog does not hit him, otherwise it will take a lot of effort and much time to regain the dog's confidence. This part of the exercise should be included in the training each day before increasing the distance between you and the dog while he is in the stay position. Each time you return to the dog, after having left him in the down and stay positions, walk past him or circle him by stepping over him, otherwise as you approach him he may get up when you do not want him to. He *must* wait for the next command.

After about a week it should be possible for you to leave the dog in the stay position up to a distance of about fifty yards, and for you to pass behind small buildings, trees and other obstacles. Do, however, let the dog see you often. Then take a longer time to circle round him until eventually you can leave him for about ten to fifteen minutes. This may take as long as a month to achieve. After the dog has done the stay for about ten days, place the pin in the ground near the end of the lead, but not in the loop, to make him think he is still tethered. Then, several days later, abandon the use of the pin. If you are not absolutely certain that the dog will remain in the stay position, tie the long line to the end of the lead, and if the dog should decide to get up and run off the line will be long enough for you to grab hold of to get him back quickly.

For those who wish to, practise the above in the sitting, standing, and any other position, with the appropriate commands and signals, and start by stepping over the dog, swinging the lead round him, and so on. It all adds to the discipline.

Having mastered this exercise so far, take the dog to different localities and, later, into the street, tying him to railings if necessary, and practise leaving him for short periods. Insist on his being in the down and stay positions whenever you stop to talk to people. Sooner or later some dear old lady, also with a dog, will call out to you 'Is your dog all right?'

Don't let it worry you, just put your dog down, say 'Stay', place your foot over the lead, and ask the person to pass on, as you are training the dog. It may take you a few more minutes to get to your destination, but as you are training your dog to take no notice of other people, such people unknowingly are assisting you.

'DEAD'
This is the command to the dog when you want him to lie on his right side.

The main object of this exercise is to get the dog in a position that will allow you to examine his underparts, including his feet, to ascertain whether he has any sores, cuts, thorns and so on that require attention, without your having to struggle with him unnecessarily. It also impresses people with the discipline a handler has over his dog, but this is only incidental.

The dog should be placed in the down position to begin this exercise. The handler stands at the head of and facing the dog, and makes sure that the dog's legs are not likely to impede him as he rolls over on to his right side. In other words, see that the back leg on that side in particular is tucked under the body. Bending slightly over the dog, the handler takes a grip on the middle of the lead with his left hand and draws the lead as far as he can towards the left, at the same time using his

'Speak'. Holding a piece of meat, raise the right hand quickly upwards from the centre of the body, jerk on the lead with the left hand and take half a pace backwards saying 'speak'. Use this as the signal to 'speak'.

'Heel'. Sit the animal on your left side and, with either lead or line held in both hands, walk slowly. Stop after about six paces, make the dog sit by jerking the lead upwards, and then repeat. The lead should be twisted round the right hand and held lightly in the left.

'*Down*'. Hold the lead in the left hand, a far as possible to your left. Raise th right hand above the head . . .

. . . strike the middle of the lead smartly with the right hand . . .

. . . forcing the le downwards until the d is 'down'. Later use t action without the le as the signal to go 'dow

right hand to push the dog's chest gently so that his whole body rolls over on to his right side. To give the dog confidence, start by feeling his tummy all over, and his legs, as though to soothe him, with the right hand. But keep the lead taut while you are doing this since with a dog experiencing this for the first time you can never be sure that he will like it, and if he doesn't he will struggle and may bite. The few seconds given to tautening the lead in the left hand may enable you to draw away the right hand in time to avoid a bite. With a difficult dog use a muzzle until you are confident he won't bite.

Practise this several times during obedience training, making the dog roll over as described until he knows what is expected of him each time you command him to go dead. Gradually give up pushing him over so that he obeys the order when you give him the signal by motioning the right hand from your right to your left side. Eventually cease holding the lead in the left hand and use the signal with the right hand only.

To perfect this exercise, use the long line, stand farther away from the dog until you can command him to go dead from a dozen yards or so and can rely on him to be left in this position for several minutes. The word of command 'Dead' should be slurred whenever you want the dog to adopt this position, no word, of course, being used when the signal only is given.

'STAND'

This is the command to the dog when he is in the sit, down, or any other position and you want him to stand on his four feet.

To make a dog stand and remain in that position for several minutes begin the exercise with the dog in the sit position.

Stand in front of the dog with the lead in the left hand and draw him towards you gently. At the same time use the word of command 'Stand', gently, and slur the word. If the dog does not readily stand, place your left foot under his belly

D

and slowly raise him into the stand position. An alternative method is to raise him with your left hand under his belly, the lead being transferred to the right hand. Whichever method you use *do* make him stand. Gently place the lead on the animal's back if you feel confident by now that he will stand and not attempt to move off. If there is a tendency for the dog to disobey, then retain the lead in your right hand and gently stroke his back from head to tail, and circle round him.

During this period repeat the command several times to instil in the dog this word of command. Afterwards you can make the signal to stand by pointing to the dog with the forefinger of the right hand, palm upwards, and drawing the hand towards you almost as though you were calling him to hand. This cannot be done, of course, until you have found it unnecessary to use the lead to induce the dog to come towards you and to stand. The hand action is similar to that used in drawing in the lead, as described above.

The method of placing the left foot under the dog to make him stand is preferable to placing the hand there because, in the standing position, you will be able to anticipate any movement the dog is likely to make, whereas if you have one hand under the dog and you are stooping, you are not in a favourable position if the dog decides to move off or attempts to snap at you.

Having got the dog to stand, try to step over him and, if necessary, have the long line attached to the lead just in case he should attempt to run off. From now on circle the dog and increase the distance from him according to the confidence you have in him at this stage.

Practise making the dog stand a yard or so away from you, the line attached to his collar, and gently pull him towards you as you did with the lead. Later, increase the distance, and again, after several weeks, do the exercise without the line.

As soon as you have made the dog familiar with the command and mode of standing, walk with him heeling on your left, then stop slowly and command him to stand, at the same time adding tension to the lead with the left hand. When the dog stands, walk round him saying, 'Stand, stand', repeating this routine several times, since he may, if not instructed, try to walk round with you. When you feel that he will stand on command, gently lay the lead on his back and walk away several yards. Then, when you call him to heel, praise him and repeat the whole procedure.

After a few days it should be quite easy to introduce variations when making the dog stand. For instance, I try to jump over my dogs in order to make them steady. I also make one dog jump over another, thus getting dog used to dog.

'FETCH' (and 'DROP')

This is the command when the handler wishes the dog to fetch an object to him that may or may not be in sight, and to drop it on command.

The leather collar only should be used for this exercise. In the initial stages, if the dog receives a jerk on his neck, as will certainly happen if a choke, chain collar is used, he may never learn to retrieve. Similarly, if you impede the line accidentally and the dog gets a sudden jolt on his neck it may take him days to recover from the experience. Take care that nothing of this kind is likely to happen. Use the word 'Fetch' for each retrieve.

Put the dog on a long line, sitting on your left. Have a cloth rolled into a ball (about the size of a tennis ball) wound tightly round with string. I generally use the cloth bag, described earlier, with the sling wound round it, in the initial stages.

With the right hand, indicate several times with the ball, in front of the dog's nose, that you are going to throw it. This will attract the dog's attention, and then throw the ball gently about three yards, not more. Allow the dog to run after it and, if possible, get him to bring it back to you. As soon as the dog runs for the ball let the rope line, which should always be on your left side for this exercise, run through your left hand held as high as possible, the line being allowed to run through the 'V' made by the thumb and forefinger. Then, after the dog has picked up the ball, use both hands on the line, hand over hand, and draw him back to you. Make the dog, still holding the ball, sit in front of you and drop it into your right hand on the command 'Drop'. *Do* reward the dog. The meat titbit soon encourages the dog to give up the ball for the meat.

Having practised this for several days it should be possible to increase the 'throw' to the full length of the line, but it must be left to the handler's discretion to decide when to throw the ball farther away. In other words, it is not much good increasing the length of throw if the dog fails or hesitates to pick up the ball and bring it back to his handler.

After a week or so you should be able to leave the dog in the down position and walk several yards away—the dog still, of course, on the line—put the ball on the ground, and walk back to the dog. Motion with the right hand in the direction of the ball and direct the dog to 'Fetch'. Every time the dog brings you the ball make him sit in front of you for a few minutes, and drop the article into your hand on command.

By this time you will probably have tried the fetch with several different objects. That is all to the good, but I am not in favour of teaching a dog to fetch or carry metal or glass objects, as metal can produce sharp edges like a knife and razor, and glass is too easily broken. Either can cause serious injury.

After the dog has mastered this part of the exercise hide the ball and ask him to fetch it. Do this in long grass a short distance away to start with, then increase the distance. Later, get an assistant to hide the object a minute or so before you arrive on the scene, and ask the dog to fetch. He will take about a month to become perfect. Eventually, have several articles hidden for the dog to retrieve, and be sure to reward the dog each time he brings you one of the articles.

Never ask a dog to retrieve more than three times in one day, and always end on a successful retrieve; the dog will be all the more eager to retrieve on the following day if this policy is followed. The chances are that if you ask the dog to retrieve more often than I have suggested, you will tire him out or he will become bored, and if as a result he fails to retrieve you will have been wasting your time. It is a good rule never to ask a dog to do anything more than three times in one day if he is expected to use skill and initiative, especially with seeks. He is rather like a child in this respect; you can give a child one, two or sometimes three sums to do, but when the child tires it is best to change the subject to something else.

Many dogs find it difficult to fetch an article or are reluctant to do so, possibly from being checked as puppies from chewing carpets or picking up articles in the house. Examine the dog's mouth; it may be his teeth are defective or that part of his mouth is malformed, making it difficult or painful for him to pick things up and carry them. If it is any of these troubles, consult your vet, he may be able to remedy them.

With this type of animal a considerable amount of patience is required, and any headway made at all should be immediately rewarded with a piece of meat and much praise. If the dog leaves you and only smells the article, then you will have made some progress. Place a piece of meat in the article so that the dog can smell it, and get it, repeat the procedure twice more, then wait until the following day. Next time place the meat inside the article again so that he cannot get at it but stays smelling it until you give the meat to him. The dog will probably hold the article from you; let him do so and reward him with another piece of meat held in your free hand.

Sometimes, if the dog is hesitant in bringing the article back to the handler, it encourages the dog, after he has picked up the article, if the handler trots backwards a little way.

This exercise is useful when searching premises for stolen property, but remember that if a dog gives tongue when he has found an object and does not bring it back but stays where he is, he has still achieved his purpose. It is possible that the object is too big or bulky for him to carry or it is too high up for him to get at.

The handler should take advantage from the very beginning of this exercise to motion with his right and left hands the direction in which he wishes the dog to retrieve, as a guide to the dog to cover all the ground required. The dog will certainly look back towards the handler many times for that guidance, and encouraging him by pointing in the direction he is to go, and saying 'Fetch', will not only put him on the track but also increase his enthusiasm.

'CARRY'

The command 'Carry' is not usually given as a command. It is an extension of the previous exercise 'Fetch', the concluding 'Drop' being delayed until the dog has completed the 'carry' to his handler's requirements.

Begin this exercise when the dog has completely mastered the previous exercise on fetch under all conditions. Instead of taking the article from the dog when he returns to you, hold him on the lead or line and trot with him in any convenient direction. Be gentle in your actions and try to anticipate when the dog intends to drop the article on the ground, and before he does, place your right hand under the article as you direct him to drop it. Praise and reward him.

After trotting a few times with the dog carrying the article, and commanding him to 'Carry', try to reduce the pace to a slow walk. You will not be able to do this for a day or so, and it may be necessary to trot with the dog several times after your first success, to encourage him, but once he has really begun to carry it should not be long before he fully understands what the exercise is all about.

Use the small bag previously referred to and place several small articles inside it. You will, more often than not, be able to put all the working tools in it and make the dog carry this when he is returning to his kennel. The sling attached to the bag can be used to tie its opening to prevent anything falling out. Do make the bag as small as possible, otherwise you may find the dog will want to play with it. Again, it is easier for the dog to carry if the sling is wound tightly round it. The dog should now be encouraged by using the word 'Carry' to carry any suitable article in his mouth. First on the lead, then later off, but he should remain at heel.

It is a good principle to get the dog to carry because you will find that while he is doing that he is less likely to indulge in bad habits such as pulling on the lead, taking notice of other dogs, and so on.

If, when selecting a dog for police work, on enquiry you learn that the dog will carry, you can be fairly sure that he will also hold on to a sleeve in criminal work. The dog that will not carry invariably makes a poor dog for this type of work.

'Up'

This is the command given to a dog when he is required to jump over a hurdle or other obstacle.

Use the leather collar on the dog during all these exercises.

Take the dog to a low obstacle about twelve inches high. It should be a wooden one and unlikely to hurt him if he fails to clear it. At the same time that you command the 'Up', gently draw him over the jump and let him see and smell a piece of meat held in the free hand. In the initial stages it may be necessary for you to step over the low jumps with the dog.

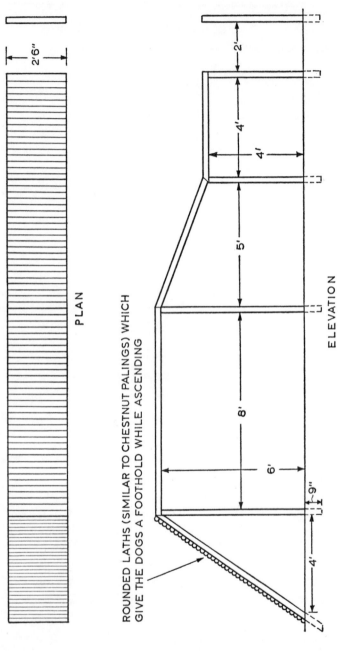

PLAN

ROUNDED LATHS (SIMILAR TO CHESTNUT PALINGS) WHICH
GIVE THE DOGS A FOOTHOLD WHILE ASCENDING

ELEVATION

Fig. 1. Bridge-type of jump enables the dog to scramble, then walk over and jump to the ground. The timber used to make the posts is about 3 inches thick, of the rustic type, and let into the ground. The slats are nailed close together and are about 2 feet 6 inches long. Take care no spaces are left between the slats or else the dog's feet may get caught up and put him off the jump. The apparatus should be as rigid as possible.

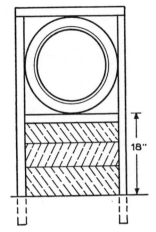

Fig. 2. A motor-tyre jump should be about 18 inches above the ground.

18"

Do this several times over the same obstacle. The dog should jump in the same direction on each occasion and be rewarded, to begin with, each time he completes the jump. A dog soon acquires the knack of jumping over small, prepared jumps, the height of which should be increased after several days. Do not, however, try to exceed more than a height of four feet or he may injure himself. Use the command 'Up' often, so that he fully understands its meaning.

Next, have several jumps of different heights and kinds formed in a circle of about forty yards so that the dog becomes familiar with all sorts of obstacles. A popular type of jump is about six feet high, eight feet long at the top and two feet six inches in width, constructed like a bridge as shown in the sketch. It has a ramp at one end to enable the dog to scramble to the top, and at the other there is a platform about four feet from the ground from which he can jump safely (Fig. 1).

Old motor tyres also make useful jumps for the dog. They are placed about two feet above the ground (*see* Fig. 2) and he can be taught to jump through them. Almost any kind of obstacle can be used provided it will not cause injuries or be likely to fall on him. Wood is best, and wire netting must be avoided.

In the pursuit of a criminal it may be necessary to assist a dog over a wall or fence that is just a little too high or awkward for him to clear. Here it is useful to teach him either to jump into your arms or over your back as a stage in finally clearing the obstacle. To accomplish this, take the dog to a wall or post, have the lead in your left hand and a small piece of meat in the right. Place your right foot against the wall or post about one foot from the ground, and draw him over your leg, at the same time giving him the command 'Up'. Give him the meat when he has cleared your leg. It will be best to use the right leg only and to ask the dog to jump only in one direction, that is from your left to your right. If you are left-handed, of course, you must practise in the way that is most convenient to you.

When the dog understands, both on and off the lead, to jump over your right leg, stand away from the post or wall, about twelve inches to start with, and raise your leg for him to jump over. Then take the dog away from the post and get him to jump over your right leg anywhere, if necessary encouraging him by drawing him over with the lead. Now teach him to jump over your right arm when it is resting against the post or wall, then, later, without the post or wall, just as you did when teaching him to jump over your leg, drawing him over with the lead at first, and always rewarding him when he is successful.

It will be noticed that, if he is jumping from your left to your right, the dog reaches the highest part of his trajectory as he is going over your right arm or leg. If, however, he is jumping in the same direction but over your left leg or arm he has reached this maximum trajectory before clearing the jump, and it is then impossible to catch him in mid air.

After the dog has succeeded in jumping over your right arm held against the post, place your left arm about twelve inches above the right and try to get him to jump through the gap between the arms. Then, gradually narrow the gap and make him jump through it. Dispense with the post altogether as soon as you can. While the dog is actually in flight you will find that by drawing your arms to your body you can catch him in them. Sometimes it may be necessary to use the post or wall again before the dog completely understands what is required, and generally it takes about a month before he becomes perfect. Practise with him on a platform such as that shown in Fig. 1, while he is in your arms. He will then get used to being handled in this way and will be less likely to struggle when you have to do the real thing to assist him over an obstacle.

When you are sure the dog will jump into your arms when required you can begin teaching him to jump over your back. To do this, position the dog about two yards behind you. Turn to your left, stoop down, bending your knees, and extend your left arm in front of you parallel to the ground. Now look over your left shoulder at the dog and place your right hand, containing a piece of meat, just above the left elbow about six inches from that arm. Ask the dog to 'Up', and he should jump over the left arm, and be given the meat. Practise several times. When the dog has mastered this stage, again place him two yards behind you, and again preferably in the down position because he seems able to spring up better from there. Now bend over with your back towards him, and this time extend both arms in the form of a 'V', and he should jump over your back when directed. Keep your head low, otherwise he may step on it in flight.

For a dog that hesitates to jump over a handler's back after qualifying so far, it is best to get an assistant to take the dog's lead to encourage him in performing the operation. It may be necessary for the assistant to draw him over the handler's back until he knows exactly what is required.

Now get near a wall so that when you bend down the wall is just a bit higher, and entice the dog to make use of your back to surmount the obstacle, the assistant helping to begin with, if necessary.

Do make sure that whenever you ask a dog to jump on strange ground it will always be possible for him to land safely, and do not expect him to clear chestnut fencing or barbed wire or anything that is likely to hurt him.

The dog can now be taught to retrieve over obstacles and, later, to swim across water for that purpose.

Use the line attached to the dog's collar in the initial stages only, again taking care not to impede the line. A portable jump should be erected, and constructed so that it will not collapse. The most practical contraption is a fence with two wings at right-angles bound together by rope. The height of this obstacle should be about two and a half feet by six feet wide, the wings being of similar dimensions. The wings, in addition to acting as supports for the jump, also prevent him from trying to side-track it.

Put the dog inside this semi-compound, take up position on the far side of the jump, and keep hold of the line. The object to be retrieved is placed some two or three yards away on the ground on your side of the fence. Call to the dog, 'Fetch', guiding the dog if necessary with the line to make him jump directly over the obstacle. When he has learnt to do this, take your stand beside him inside the semi-compound and direct him to fetch. This time the dog has to jump twice, going for, and coming back with the article. Do not forget to motion with the right hand the direction in which you want him to fetch.

Take the lesson a step further by getting him to jump over two or three obstacles and to retrieve two or three objects, but do not try to do everything at once. Build it up step by step.

'No'
This is the word of command used to correct a dog that is doing, or is about to do, something it shouldn't.

The reaction of a dog to the command 'No' depends on the handler or the owner. If the owner/handler means what he says, the dog responds accordingly. It should be used with emphasis when the dog is doing something contrary to his master's or handler's wishes, and he must be made to understand that whatever mis-activity he is up to must stop immediately. The word used must always be the same one, and no alternatives such as 'Don't', 'Stop it', or an oath substituted. If he is doing something particularly annoying you may possibly use an oath, but not as a substitute for 'No'. Probably it is the first disciplinary word that every animal should learn from its owner. Even a cat understands it, and more often than not can be made to obey it.

'KENNEL'
This is the word of command to direct the dog to go into his kennel, box or whatever form of housing has been provided for him.

This word of command should be made use of on every occasion the dog is directed to go into his kennel.

Some dogs can be persuaded to enter a kennel the first time they are ordered to do so simply by throwing a small piece of meat into it, the word of command being used at the same time. If you have managed to get the dog to go into the kennel the first time, place your left leg against the entrance and thus prevent him from coming out again. Remain so for a minute or two, and if the dog struggles to get out rap it on the nose with the middle of the lead. Do *not* use the metal parts of the lead. Then, while the dog is hesitating whether or not to disobey, stand about a yard away and continue to prevent him from coming out by striking the lead against the entrance of the kennel, the dog's nose or another part of his body. Keep repeating the command 'Kennel' while this is going on.

Another effective method is to tie the dog to the kennel chain, take hold of his collar with the left hand, and with the right hand grip the dog's tail and push him head first into the kennel, lifting him up if necessary, the word of command being repeated all the time you are doing this. The dog should then be kept there as explained above.

Sometimes a dog is either too strong or just too much for the handler to manage, an occurrence that often happens when a dog has been taken over from someone else's care. In this event it will be necessary, after he is tied to the kennel chain, to run the long line through the 'D' of the collar so that the handler can hold both ends of the line at the same time. The ends are then passed through the entrance of the kennel and under the far end of the sliding roof, which is slightly opened for that purpose. The dog is then literally pulled into his kennel. One end of the rope can then be released, the handler pulling the line free by the other end. Take care that the end that is pulled is that with the swivel on it. In the meantime the handler takes up position in front of the kennel and blocks the entrance with his leg, the procedure then being continued as before.

Whichever method proves best, the dog will take a day or so to understand. After that it is quite simple to direct the dog to go into his kennel when required, but it should be practised *every time* the dog is brought back to his quarters.

The principle is much the same if you wish the dog to understand that he is to enter his box or lie on his mat in the house. Tie him with the lead or chain within reach of his box or mat and make him stay where you wish him to take up his quarters. Leave him tied up for several nights, and always use the word of command you wish to employ when ordering him to go to his box or mat.

Making a dog stay in any particular part of a car as soon as he enters the vehicle is quite easy to accomplish by having a short lead or rope permanently anchored in that part of the car, and fastening the dog there. For ease in tying, a spare lead clip attached to the rope will help. The dog will adopt his seat after a week or so of such training. The lead or rope used in this way also acts as a safety-belt for him and will prevent his falling on the driver or other occupants if the vehicle has to come to an emergency stop.

Never allow the dog, as is often seen, to put his nose out of the window when the car is in motion; it will impair his smelling abilities, and it is dangerous.

'QUIET'
This is the word of command used for a dog that tends to give tongue for no justifiable reason.

It is necessary to instil this command in every dog, particularly those that yowl in the middle of the night for no sensible reason, including baying at the moon.

With the dog that is tied to a kennel the matter is comparatively simple. A shot or two from a catapult, even on the sides of the kennel, is enough to quieten it, and it can be repeated if necessary, which is seldom. Make sure, however, that you hit the hindquarters of the dog, if you have to hit him at all, and never when he is looking at you, for obvious reasons.

At the same time that the dog or kennel receives the impact of the shot, loudly exclaim, 'Quiet, quiet!' (*see* also p. 100.)

The average dog soon learns respect for the catapult, and merely to draw the catapult elastic and let it go is usually enough to quieten a noisy dog, especially after it has once felt the effect of it.

Some dogs, however, require more stringent treatment, but this ought not to arise in a dog chosen for security work; for instance, as a last resort, the use of a muzzle.

The opportunity of teaching a dog to be quiet often arises during the lessons on making a dog 'speak'. The animal is often over-keen, but if the word 'Quiet' is used incisively and repeated several times the dog is momentarily taken aback and quite soon learns its meaning by comparison, as is the way with human beings.

If the dog is out walking on the lead and decides to start barking at another animal, a sharp pull on the lead, if it is wearing the choke, chain collar, often has the desired effect, or a sharp rap on the hindquarters with the ring end of the lead may be similarly effective, together with the command 'Quiet'.

2

Security Training

'STOP HIM'
This is the command given by a handler when he wishes a dog to chase, stop, and hold a suspected criminal.

The initial training for this exercise is included in the 'Introduction' under the heading 'Selecting a Dog for Security Work', pp. 14 to 18, and will not be repeated here.

After the dog has provided evidence that he will hold on to a sack whenever he is required to do so, the sack should be wrapped round the right arm of an assistant, who will act as a suspected criminal. If the dog has a strong bite be sure to include one of a pair of leather leggings, or even a pair, under the sack wrapped round the man's arm. You can ascertain the 'bite' of the dog by his age, size, and, particularly by his tenacity when holding a sack. His previous history will also tell you a good deal.

Tie the dog to a fence, get the assistant to gauge the distance the dog can travel from the fence before being pulled up by the limit of the lead, and to stand almost at that distance. Now tell him to shake the protected arm only, in front of the dog. If the dog goes for the assistant's arm, as he should, let him hold on to it for several seconds, encouraged by the handler if necessary. The handler then commands 'Cease' or 'Down', takes hold of the dog by the collar and draws him off the arm, praising him enthusiastically with 'Good boy', 'Well done',

E

and so on. Repeat the procedure, say, three times, then attach the dog to the long line instead of the lead.

Now let the 'suspect' stand three or four yards away, hold the line in your left hand, make quite sure the line is not likely to be impeded, and that the dog is on your left side facing the suspect. Next, ask the suspect to shake his protected arm up and down to attract the dog, and while he does so point towards him with the right hand, command the dog to 'Stop him', and at the same time let the line slide through the left hand. The right hand should be ready to grip the line at any time if the dog should attempt to get round behind the assistant.

It is most important that the line does not become entangled at this stage, otherwise the assistant may get bitten. The handler must be able to gauge the distance the dog can travel, not only because he must be ready to prevent the dog running round behind the assistant or jumping up at his face, but also because when the dog gets a hold on the suspect's arm, it must not at the same time receive a jerk on its neck, otherwise it may be put off this exercise. Do be most careful to estimate correctly the distance the rope may be allowed to pass through the hand. Finally, command the dog off, as described. Practise the above about three times a day for three successive days.

At this stage the assistant may find it expedient to grasp the rope a yard or so from the neck of the dog with the left hand, which will enable him to keep the rope away from his feet and prevent its becoming entangled. The handler, of course, must relinquish his hold on the line while the assistant is holding it. *Never allow a dog to run with the lead attached to the collar. If the ring at the end of the lead hits his genitals the dog will never chase again.*

The next step is an extension of the last exercise. While the dog is holding on to his arm the assistant should cry out as though hurt, and at the same time pull the dog on his arm up and down and, if possible, allow himself to be pulled towards the dog. This is done to ensure that the dog is getting a proper hold. Repeat about three times, then stop. Do the same thing for three or four days running.

It is most important that you do not tire the dog at this stage or continue the exercise for too long. Always end on a good note. You will be surprised how eager the dog will be to do this work if you take your time in the initial stages. Always make things easy for him; later, he will take the hard work in his stride. When you are quite sure and satisfied that the dog will hold on to the 'suspect', and only then, get the assistant to increase the distance from the dog by about ten yards. Go through the same procedure as above. After this increase the distance to about twenty yards, over the period of about a week, but make sure that the dog will chase and hold the assistant at every increase in distance.

Releasing the 'Bite'

It is just as important to teach the dog to release his hold of the arm as it is to teach him to hold the arm when commanded to do so. This can be achieved by various methods.

One is for the handler to offer the dog a piece of meat by placing it beside his nose with the left hand, as is sometimes necessary with a dog that is on the keen side in the initial stages. At the same time, the handler draws the dog off with the line in his right hand, closely observing the moment that the dog releases his bite to take the meat so that the dog can be prevented from taking a second hold.

A second method is for the handler to grasp the dog's collar with the left hand as he is swung round in a clockwise direction by the assistant, and to grab the root of the animal's tail with the right hand, giving it a gentle twisting. The handler must take care that when he grasps the dog's collar he gets a firm grip, otherwise the dog will surely attempt to bite him.

As the dog is being swung by the assistant in a clockwise direction the handler from now on should always approach the assistant from the opposite side, i.e. from an anticlockwise direction. If he does not, the handler may find that he is chasing the dog round the assistant. The assistant is able to help the handler in the initial stages by almost placing the dog into his hands when the handler is taking the dog off.

If the dog is too much for the handler to manage at this stage, as sometimes happens with a nervous handler who is not quite sure of himself or the dog, then the best method is for the handler to hit the dog on its back with the end of the lead. The handler should, of course, have a firm grip on the line in his left hand, to draw the dog off as he employs his right to strike the dog.

Any method practised should be done with the command 'Cease' or 'Down', and it will be appreciated that this will always have to be done several times before the dog will understand and release the arm when directed to do so. Soon, the dog will understand that when the handler grasps his collar and, at the same time, gives the word of command, he is to release his hold. Eventually, all that will be necessary will be the word of command for the dog to stand away from his 'suspect'. A word of advice here: the handler should be up beside the suspect before he instructs the dog to release his hold. If he should direct the dog to release his hold when he is only halfway towards the suspect, and the dog should let go, the suspect may attempt to make off and escape. It is good policy to touch the suspect before giving directions to the dog, especially during training, the handler thus forming a habit that the dog understands.

The commands 'Cease' and 'Down' are alternatives. Some handlers prefer 'Cease' when taking a dog off the arm, but I prefer 'Down' because it is a command the animal has already been taught during the obedience training, and has become

'*Stay*'. Start with the dog in the 'down' position and with his lead pinned to the ground. Step over the dog, swinging the folded line round him. Repeat several times with the distance between you and the dog increased until eventually the steel pin is dispensed with. Practise also in the 'sit' position. The word of command 'stay' should be repeated many times.

'*Stand*'. From the 'sit' position, draw the dog towards you with the lead in the left hand and the forefinger of the right hand inducing the dog to stand. Later use this sign without the lead.

Teaching a dog to go 'dead'. Have the dog in the 'down' position, draw the lead to your left and force him over with the right hand.

'*Dead*' position completed.

'*Fetch*'. Shake the folded bag in front of the dog's nose several times, then throw it about five or six paces in front of him so that he retrieves it. The line is held slack in the left hand and used to draw the dog with bag in mouth towards you.

familiar with during initial training. But it really doesn't matter which word is used so long as the dog acts immediately and releases his hold on the suspect.

Recalling the Dog

I am sometimes asked if a dog should be taught to go 'Down' when halfway towards a suspect, or to return to the handler if the handler realises that the suspect is not the man he wants and, perhaps, an innocent party. My answer is: the handler should never put himself in such a dilemma. He should be quite sure that the person he wants the dog to stop is the right one. One does not fire a gun at someone and expect the bullet to come back if, after firing it, it is realised that the wrong person has been aimed at—neither should a dog be ordered to stop the wrong man. However, to satisfy those who think such a mistake is excusable, the general procedure will be explained. Personally I have never made an error of this kind, and would not condone it for the additional reason that a dog will lose his incentive to chase if he becomes aware that he may suddenly be directed to go down, or to return. It is done in competitions, mainly to give variation to the events, and it may look impressive, but it is not good practice.

The method is as follows. The long line is attached to the dog, sitting at the handler's left side. The assistant paces off the approximate distance the line will allow the dog to run, he adds about another ten paces, marks that distance, and returns to a yard or so from the handler and dog. The assistant then shakes his protected arm up and down and runs slowly off in the direction of the mark he has previously made. The handler directs the dog to 'Stop him'. Approximately halfway the handler yells out 'Down' to the dog. If the animal does not obey, he is pulled up by the line, and again ordered to go down. To make the dog return, the handler orders the dog to hand and draws him by the line if necessary. It takes a dog several days to get used to the idea of stopping halfway, and inevitably he shows a tendency to slow down as he is approaching the assistant because of an expected jerk on his neck. To try to get over this difficulty, about every third time he is directed to chase and hold the assistant, the dog should be allowed to stop and hold his quarry.

Take the exercise a step further by increasing the distance, placing the line as far as it will go from the handler and dog in the direction the assistant will run, and pegging the end of it in the ground with the iron pin. The assistant must again pace the distance, this time about three times the length of the line, and make a mark with his foot (or he can place a marker on the ground; anything so long as he knows how far he has to run). He then returns to dog and handler. The assistant now runs off and, as he is approaching his mark, the dog is directed to 'Stop him', and when it has reached halfway the handler again calls to the dog 'Down'. The line pulls the dog up if it is too enthusiastic in trying to get at the assistant, after which it is called to hand by the handler.

Rewarding the dog with titbits sometimes induces the dog to return when called to hand, but as it is the chase the dog really enjoys it is expecting rather much of him to be pleased at being recalled.

Stopping One Person

Training must include teaching the dog to stop one particular person and to prevent its chasing the wrong person, particularly when there are other people about as will certainly occur when using dog patrols in parks or other open spaces. A considerable amount of practice is, of course, necessary, and the correct moment must be chosen before ordering the dog to pursue and stop any particular person. Again, much depends on the ability of the handler. Once the dog has been taught to chase, stop and hold a person as previously described, instruct another assistant, without a protective sleeve, to stand and keep perfectly still halfway along the route you intend the dog to take, that is, about fifty yards away from the handler and dog. The 'suspect' is about fifty yards farther on, wearing protective covering on his right arm, which he should wave up and down and, at the same time, yell out in defiance.

At a signal from the handler the suspect begins to run at a slow pace, at approximately forty-five degrees from left to right of the path along which the dog will approach him. The handler uses his right hand to point in the direction of the running suspect, but he must point from the dog's nose. The handler calls on the suspect to stop, and, of course, he takes no notice but immediately quickens his pace, which will help to attract the dog's attention. The handler directs the dog to 'Stop him' and it will be found that the dog will take no notice of the assistant standing halfway.

On the next run the assistant who was at first standing halfway now walks slowly across the path of the dog, and the dog will again ignore him. Next, have two assistants in the path of the dog, first standing still, then walking. They should stand as the dog approaches them the first time, after which they can walk. Introduce a third assistant, to stand with the other two, approximately halfway along the path the dog will take to chase his quarry. This time let the first assistant throw his cap or some other soft material at the dog immediately the animal passes him, and the other assistants can also throw something at the dog on the next run as the dog passes them. Later sticks can be thrown at the dog, some of which should be aimed to fall in front of the dog to slacken the animal's pace, but do this only when the dog has become very efficient at chasing a person, which will be, approximately, after about a month's training.

During these several chases the 'suspect' should also throw in the path of the dog an article such as a handbag or tin pail, to hinder the dog approaching him. This will make the dog used to having things thrown at him in the course of his chase.

The dog will now be quite used to people crossing his path, and something more realistic can be introduced.

Select a suitable spot where there are bushes or a wall that a potential thief might choose to hide behind, and get an assistant, with his right arm protected, to take up position there before bringing the dog on to the scene. Now get another assistant, the 'victim', to walk off in the direction of the hidden 'thief', carrying a bag or attaché case. As he passes the spot where the thief is hidden, the latter runs up behind him, snatches the bag, gives the 'victim' a shove in any direction, and makes off.

The 'victim' calls loudly for help and waves his hands about frantically. The dog and handler have been witnesses of the 'snatch', and immediately the handler releases the dog, who makes for the 'thief' and stops him, passing the shouting 'victim' *en route*. The handler now joins dog and thief, and all three go back to the 'victim', other assistants crowding round. The 'thief' should now try to make a 'get-away', some of the assistants contriving to impede the dog in its renewed efforts to 'stop' the thief, which it will succeed in doing without any additional command from its handler.

During exercises of this kind the dog's sole idea is to catch and stop the person who is running; therefore, if by calling 'Stop' you can incite that person to run, the dog will immediately react as you want him to. It is most important that when the handler points towards the 'criminal' the pointed finger starts from the dog's nose and then extends towards the 'criminal', and that the dog is trained until he understands that he must go only for the person at whom the finger points.

Protecting Dog and Handler
The preceding steps in training a dog to stop and hold a

'criminal' have assumed that the latter will not offer too much resistance. The following exercises teach the dog how to protect himself and his handler if the suspect shows more determination in trying to make a get-away.

Earlier, on p. 58, a procedure was described in which the dog was swung round in a clockwise direction while it was holding on to an assistant's arm. There the clockwise swing was apparently for the benefit of the assistant, but the following will demonstrate that, in fact, it was merely the initial step in teaching a dog to avoid injury.

Get the assistant to swing the dog round in a clockwise direction, and from this time onwards he must do the same thing every time the dog is given the command 'Stop him'. It is essential that while the dog is swung round on the protected arm his feet should not leave the ground since, should he release his hold, he might suffer injury either to feet or legs. The action, although instigated by the assistant during training, is actually copied by the dog when he is fully trained, so that, when he is commanded to 'Stop him', he seizes the suspect's arm and tries to swing him round and round in a clockwise direction. In doing so it makes it difficult, if not impossible, for the suspect to kick the dog or hit him with a stick. Thus, the dog learns to avoid injury from the suspect who, in turn, often becomes dizzy from being whirled round and round, and easier for the handler to deal with.

To attain this desirable objective, proceed by directing the dog to stop him, in the usual way, after the assistant has run a distance of about twenty yards. When the dog has taken hold of the assistant, the latter then swings the dog round in a clockwise direction and, with his left foot, gently at first, kicks at the dog's right side, then more forcibly, but not so fiercely as to make the dog release his hold. Later, the assistant should employ a stick in the same way, instead of the foot. After practising this several times it will be found that the assistant, instead of having to swing the dog round, will himself be swung round by the dog, who will be trying to avoid being either hit or kicked.

This part of the dog's training is essential if it is to be employed in tackling a real criminal, who will almost certainly be armed with a stick or other weapon. It also assists the handler in getting the dog off the criminal's arm. The handler, as previously mentioned, should approach from an anti-clockwise direction.

The dog is now taught to protect the handler, and here he is eventually expected to act on his own, whenever the occasion may arise. The dog, of course, must be assisted in the initial stages. Have the assistant run away from you, waving his arm up and down all the time he is running until he is about twenty yards away. Order the dog 'Stop him', and as he obeys, run up to the assistant, order the dog to cease his hold, and to go down about two yards from the 'suspect'. Speak to the assistant loudly, as though questioning a suspect on what he is doing, and walk slowly round him, running your hand about him as though searching him. These actions will instil in the dog the necessity of keeping his eye on the quarry, and prepare him for the next part of the exercise.

When you are between the assistant and dog, let the assistant push you to the ground, yell out as though hurt, and at the same time call loudly to the dog 'Stop him'. The assistant attempts to run off, not too quickly, as the dog should be given sufficient time to hold him by the arm again, and encouraged if necessary. The dog is then taken off and directed to go down as before. Repeat the procedure of searching the 'suspect', and practise the above each time the dog is directed to chase and stop that person. Later, the dog must do the holding on his own immediately. Practise with and without the command 'Stop him' until the dog acts on his own every time the assistant pushes you to the ground.

The handler can occasionally walk with the assistant on his left side, as though taking him into custody, holding him by the protected arm with the right hand. If the dog attempts to jump up and hold the protected arm, as may happen in the early stages, the handler can easily ward the animal off. After walking a little distance, get the assistant to give you a push and fall to the ground. If the 'suspect' tries to get away, he should again be stopped by the dog. Walk on another ten yards and go through the same procedure, preferably when the dog is least expecting it or is becoming less interested. It will soon be found that the dog will immediately respond, and keep close to the prisoner to prevent his trying to escape.

It will be appreciated that an assistant who runs away from a dog, or attempts to escape, should be most careful to position himself in such a way that he can offer his protected arm to the dog when it goes for him.

Do not encourage a dog to go for the legs of a quarry; should either fall, one or the other may sustain a back injury. If an assistant should ever fall on a dog during this exercise, the dog will never chase again. Dogs taught to go for the legs of a 'suspect' lend themselves open to instant injury, for a prisoner can use both arms to free himself by killing the dog. I have known cases when a person so held by a dog was able to pick up a stick and ram it down the dog's throat.

Carry this exercise a step further: the assistant being questioned by the handler, the dog in the down position about two yards away, the handler going round the 'suspect', who is waiting until the handler is between the dog and himself. Now let the suspect grab the handler round the neck with the left arm, being careful to offer the dog the protected arm, and try to swing both dog and handler round. In the struggle that is bound to follow, the handler, of course, eventually frees himself and again commands the dog to go down. This exercise will help to ensure that the dog goes to the assistance of the handler under all conditions; especially if the handler yells out on each occasion as though hurt.

As soon as you feel confident that the dog will protect you, and that he understands he has to act on his own without any word of command, take hold of your assistant, by either arm, walk him into a shed or room, and sit him on a chair or form. Order the dog to go down close to the suspect and, at the same time, say 'Watch him' (*see* below). Leave the dog and man alone, and hide yourself behind a door or screen. Acting on your instructions, after a few minutes the 'suspect' will try to get away. It doesn't matter in which direction he goes so long as he is in a position to offer the protected arm to the dog. The dog must then hold the suspect by the protected arm. It may be necessary to direct him in the initial stages, or for the assistant to encourage him, but eventually he will do it automatically. Take the dog off and praise him by saying 'Good boy' and so on. Repeat the exercise three times each day. Direct the assistant to take longer each time in trying to escape, so that dog and suspect can be left for some fifteen to twenty minutes while you pretend to be making enquiries and so on. Practise several times, treat the assistant more roughly, and pretend to struggle with him as you push him on to a chair or form. Try to make it as realistic as possible, and talk loudly as though there was a disagreement of some kind.

Chasing, Stopping, and Holding
Now practise various forms of chasing, stopping, and holding a suspect. If there is a convenient window about three feet high in a shed or room, ask the 'suspect' to enter the building and stand behind the open window, and wave his protected arm outside it, thus helping to encourage the dog, while you command the dog to 'stop him'. Keep hold of the lead as you allow the dog to approach the window and try to assist the animal through the window, passing the lead to the assistant

eft: '*Up*'. To make the dog jump into your arms, first place your right leg on a post or wall,
aw the lead upwards and induce the dog, with meat in your right hand, to jump over
ur leg. Practise later without the post, always using the word of command '*Up*'. Right:
actise as before but with the right arm extended to the post, rewarding the dog after he
s jumped.

eft: When the dog knows how to jump over your leg and arm, form both arms into a
rcle, right arm always near the ground, and induce the dog to jump through. Right: As
e dog is passing through your arms, catch him in mid-air with both arms. Repeat several
mes.

The first test to ascertain if a dog will 'hold'. A sack is shaken in front of him.

Assessing the 'hold' of a dog.

(suspect) if necessary, to enable the dog to jump through the window. The dog then grabs at the suspect's arm. Do take care to see that the dog does not injure himself when making the jump. Lift him through the window. After the dog can do this fairly easily, darken the shed inside and repeat the exercise. Practise occasionally at night time.

After about a week practising the above lessons, allow the dog to see the assistant climb through the open window when standing about twenty yards away. Allow the 'suspect' time to get inside, then direct the dog to 'Stop him'. Now increase the distance from the shed (or room) and allow the suspect longer inside the shed. Let him escape through the door before sending the dog. Reverse the procedure, by allowing the suspect to go in by the door and out of the window. Of course, you must alter the position of observation accordingly so as to give the suspect a chance.

The average dog learns to accomplish each of these exercises after about four to six weeks' training, during which it will be noticed that each part contributes something more to his understanding of what is required of him. Now practise each, in turn, and finally stage it as a complete whole, as follows.

Let your assistant appear from behind a wall, some 100 yards away, running off with a small sack filled with a few stones. Call on him to stop and, on his ignoring your command, direct the dog to stop him. The 'suspect' throws the small sack in the path of the dog just before the animal gets a grip on his arm and begins turning him round and round. Run up and order the dog off the suspect's arm, at the same time command the dog 'Down'. While searching the suspect and circling him, he knocks you down, the dog again holds on, and is again directed to 'Cease' or 'Down'. Now take the suspect to the shed or room, make him sit on a seat, leaving the dog to look after him. He attempts to escape, and again the dog stops him. (Don't forget to collect the small bag *en route* or you won't have any evidence.)

The next procedure is to teach the dog the command 'Watch him'. It is a substitute for the command 'Speak', and it is introduced in the initial stages by adding 'Watch him' to 'Speak', fairly often, eventually dropping the command 'Speak'. 'Watch him' is more impressive and is useful when trying to disperse several people who are reluctant to do so. It is generally associated with 'crowd work'.

Begin with the dog sitting at your left side. Instruct an assistant to shake his protected arm up and down and, at the same time, with a stick in his other hand to tease the dog's legs and slowly move off. As he does so, the handler directs the dog 'Speak', 'Watch him', 'Watch him', being careful to keep a firm hold of the dog on its lead. The assistant also shouts 'Watch him' several times, until the dog begins barking really loudly. Now release the dog and let him get hold of the assistant in the usual way, and then take him off. Go back to the place you started from, repeat twice more, and finish for that day.

The object of allowing the dog to chase and stop the assistant is so that the dog's attention will always be directed towards people to be dispersed, and he will generally bark louder if, occasionally, he is allowed to snap at such people. When the dog has been trained to speak like this, get several assistants to gather about twenty yards away from you, standing about a yard from each other, yelling their heads off like hooligans, and waving sticks about. Say to the dog loudly 'Watch him' several times as you approach them, and continue saying so until you are about two yards away from them and quickening your pace. Now, take hold of the lead with both hands, allow the lead to slide through the left hand, and draw it back with the right, and direct the dog, with the aid of the lead and with the command 'Watch him', to speak at each person. Begin from the right-hand person and work to the left, then from left to right. Do not allow the dog to hold on to any assistant's arm, so far. Let the dog continue barking at each, in turn, until he comes to the assistant that has the protected arm, and then allow the dog to hold on to him. Take the dog off. (The dog will, of course, have barked at him before going for his arm.)

Go back to the same starting point and this time have all the assistants wearing protective arm sleeves. Approach as before, and let the dog bark at each in turn, again beginning from the right, and after the dog has really given tongue let him chase and stop the first person he barked at. The other assistants should disperse in different directions and as you take the dog off the first criminal, direct him to stop the second one, and so on. Now get the assistants to form a small circle, question each, in turn, and as one assistant attempts to escape, the dog will stop him of his own accord.

This training is to ensure that the dog is on the alert to tackle any person trying to escape when a group of people is being questioned. The dog may be capable of stopping several people running away, but it is as well to make sure that you have arrested at least one person.

After the dog is fully conversant with the lessons on 'Watch him', try to evoke a response in him when the command is reduced to a whisper. It will need much practice and is best started when the dog has barked at a person and needs very little encouragement to bark again. In other words, say 'Watch him' in a normal voice, then, soon afterwards, whisper it.

In practice, when approaching a person and the command 'Watch him' is given in a whisper, the dog gives the impression to all around him that he is more than interested in that person. The effect, therefore, is well worth the additional effort in training. Perfection can be attained by using the whispered command frequently, the handler using his discretion on whether or not the occasion is suitable.

During the exercises on 'Stop him' it will have been noted that only the right arm is given protection, and the reader may have wondered why a full suit of protective clothing was not worn. Provided the dog has been taught each step thoroughly there is no need for any further protection, as the dog will make for the arm only. The advantages are many: the assistant can act more as a real criminal would, and a protective suit, which is bulky and heavy as well as being hot to wear, considerably limits his activities. Certainly, he cannot run easily. Further, the dog will learn to bite at any part of the body, and because the material is hard and stiff, he will release his hold after attempting to bite, and will, therefore, become a biter only, instead of learning to hold on and, also, he may become dangerous. On refresher courses, with a dog so trained, few people will be prepared to act as 'suspect', especially on 'Seeks', as they may get bitten.

The arm is a part of the body least likely to sustain permanent injury, if any. A person with a dog holding one arm is rendered half immobile and easier to deal with, especially if that arm is holding a stick or other weapon. The amount of material required for the protection of the arm is very much less than that required for a full protective suit, and is a fraction of the cost.

In the United Kingdom it is now accepted for security and police work that a dog may 'hold' an arm, but any form of savagery on the part of the dog is forbidden. In many countries, however, where life is held more cheaply, a dog is taught to savage and kill, when, of course, full protective clothing is necessary in training. The only other occasions when complete protective clothing is necessary are in competitions, where the 'quarry' cannot be certain if he will receive a bite or not.

If you are ever invited to run for a strange dog, only do so if you have seen it run for some other person first. You will then be able to judge how it is likely to act, and act accordingly yourself.

There are two other methods of stopping a person by means of a dog, and although they are not always quite so effective as those already described they should, nevertheless, be mentioned.

The first is by directing the dog to run after a person and teaching it to run round and round him barking. No attempt is made by the dog to hold the suspect. It is useful with many wrongdoers but not with all. I mention this form of stopping a suspect because it was the first method adopted by police but abandoned because it was found that some suspects just ignored the dog, and were able to make their getaway. It is, however, useful up to a point, and many women incapable of handling a dog that is trained to hold a person have had their dogs trained in this way as an alternative.

The failure of the first method to achieve its object led to the second method, which is to train the dog to run after a 'suspect' and hold on to his coat or mackintosh. This, again, proved futile with some criminals as they merely discarded their garments and left the dog literally shaking the clothing they had abandoned. Something had to be thought of that would prove completely effective, and after much consideration the hold on the arm became universally approved and adopted.

Reverting to the first method mentioned above, it is advisable to practise with a dog that has not previously been encouraged to 'hold' a person, for if the dog has been taught to 'hold', the chances are that it will possibly do so again. The giving of food plays a vital part in this exercise, and the assistant should, therefore, take with him several pieces of meat that he can readily give to the dog as required. He does not, however, need to wear any form of protective clothing. The dog should be hungry, in other words fasted for a day or so

F

before starting this exercise, and fed only during these lessons.

The handler has the dog on the line on his left side, and takes special care that the line is not likely to impede the dog as it approaches the assistant. (The line is discarded as the dog becomes proficient.) The assistant allows the dog to smell the piece of meat in his hand extended towards the dog, and he then moves off a pace or two. The dog is directed to 'Stop him' and, of course, is permitted to take the meat from the assistant immediately. This is practised three times a day at ever-increasing distances, up to about thirty yards, which will take about a week to perfect. The next procedure is to make the dog bark just before receiving the reward from the assistant. The dog, of course, must have been previously taught to 'speak'. As the dog reaches the assistant, the latter moves a pace or so round and round and waves his right hand, holding the meat, up and down, and directs the dog to speak. On the next run the assistant quickens his pace and actions when the dog arrives beside him by turning round several times in a small circle, moving either arm, if necessary, to make the dog speak, and every time the dog gives tongue he immediately rewards it. The dog is likewise praised by the handler when he also arrives beside the dog. The distance is increased from this period onwards. Less and less meat is given as a reward, then it is given only occasionally, and afterwards it will seldom be necessary.

The second method is somewhat similar to the training given to the dog when teaching it to hold the arm, but the arm is not used or even protected. Once the dog will hold on to a sack it is then encouraged to chase the person waving the sack, which is never waved above the waist. The handler moves in and directs the dog to 'Cease' or 'Down' after each time it has stopped, or taken hold of the sack held by the assistant. The distance is increased as training proceeds and it becomes second nature to the dog to act accordingly. The sack is now tied to the assistant, which is done by inserting a belt or rope through the extreme ends of the sack, and allowing the loop made by the rope or belt to hang over one shoulder, the opposite arm being slipped through that loop. The dog is then directed to 'Stop him' at that distance at which previously the dog had become proficient when the sack only was waved for him.

The next stage is to place the sack over a mackintosh or long garment worn by the assistant. The dog then practises on the combined attire. The sack is then dispensed with and the long coat only is used. As the coat or mackintosh gradually becomes shortened by being torn a short jacket is substituted, but it should be open and allowed to flap about in the first few instances. Unfortunately, the supply of garments for practising with soon becomes less and less and a sack has again to be resorted to.

This method was effective up to the point I have already mentioned and in no case did the dogs ever take hold of anything else but the clothing of the person being chased. Incidentally, both these methods are made use of in the making of films, the second one in particular because it looks effective and, as a rule, can be put into operation without harm. Actors as a rule are not over-enthusiastic when it comes to dogs going for them.

Escorting Criminals

There are several methods of escorting a criminal when on foot, after a dog and handler have stopped such a person. Several schools advocate that the prisoner should walk a few paces in front of the dog and handler, so that the dog is always in a position to stop and hold that person if the need should arise.

In practice, I generally found that by taking hold of the

criminal's right arm with my left hand I was less likely to lose him should he decide to make a getaway, my dog following on my left close behind, to give assistance if necessary.

Both methods of course are correct, and both should be practised and left to the handler to use either method.

The first method is right up to a point and would be proper when escorting a prisoner in open country, or on the parade ground, where the dog has plenty of room to act. But in a High Street, especially on a Saturday afternoon with many people about, including women pushing prams and children walking by their sides, it would be ridiculous. A prisoner would soon make up his mind to try to escape and might push a pram into the path of the handler and dog, or even run into the roadway, when possible injury to dog or handler could occur—and there would be little sympathy for a dog or handler who allowed a prisoner to escape because he was not held by the arm.

Many prisoners, of course, will give very little trouble and will walk quite quietly because of the presence of the dog.

The next question is what happens when there are several prisoners to be escorted. This, of course, must be left to the handler's discretion and tact.

'SEEK'
This is the command given when it is believed that a 'suspect' is hidden in some premises and the dog is to find him by 'direct scent'.

Begin this exercise by instructing an assistant, who is to act as the 'suspect', to take with him in a tin one pound of meat cut into small pieces. It is important to note the direction of the wind, as the dog will use the wind to scent his quarry. This method is called finding a person by 'direct scent' as opposed to ground scent.

Select a location that is partially covered with small bushes, and get the assistant to lie down behind a bush large enough to conceal him completely. On no account let the dog see the assistant go into hiding, otherwise the exercise will be useless.

Take the dog to within about twenty yards of the place where the assistant is hidden, sit the dog down by your left side, attach the long line, and pat him several times to convey to him the impression that you have every confidence in what you are about to teach him. Now walk very slowly towards the hidden quarry, and at every other step give the dog the command 'Seek, seek', accenting the double 'e'. Make sure the wind is in the right directon to assist the dog as you pass within two or three yards of the quarry. If the dog 'points' or picks up the suspect's scent or attempts to go towards him, encourage the animal to do so, and if the dog is at all slow in finding the hidden man, and if it is necessary, take the dog to him. When the dog arrives at the bush where the man is concealed, or comes on him, the 'suspect' must immediately give the dog about a third of the food in the tin. The 'suspect' may have the meat already in his hand, but the tin of meat should be closed, as it is most important that the dog should scent the perspiration of the man, not the meat, as early as possible.

Try the exercise twice over. If the dog does not do the first 'seek' well, go through the same procedure over the same ground. Otherwise, practise in a fresh area. *Do three 'seeks' a day and no more*, throughout the course of the eight weeks training.

Getting the 'suspect' to give the meat to the dog in the initial stages is highly important, the object being to instil in the dog the habit of staying with the 'suspect' and, as the dog becomes familiar with the exercise, to give tongue when he finds him. The only way this habit can be formed is for the 'suspect' to give him the meat; if the handler gives the reward, the dog will form the habit of returning to his handler as quickly as he can, thus letting the suspect get away. What the dog must have is praise from the handler, not food. Food is essential in training all animals, as any circus trainer will agree. In the three 'seeks' described above food should be given on each occasion, but after a while the food should be given on the last 'seek' only, and by the end of the course not at all; nevertheless one has to be guided by circumstances and the progress made by the dog.

Progress is measured by the dog's ability to 'seek' and find the concealed assistant at increasing distances from the zero point until successful at about a hundred yards, and by the handler being able to let the line run out as the dog becomes proficient, and, finally, allow it to drop from his hands altogether. It should take about two weeks to perfect the exercise so far.

The dog should now have a fair idea of the meaning of the word 'seek', and the next part of the training, therefore, is to allow the dog to 'seek' on his own, first with the aid of the wind, then without any assistance from the direction of the wind.

Ask the assistant to conceal himself in a bush or ditch some thirty yards away from the place where you intend to make the dog 'seek' for him. Again, the dog must not be allowed to see the assistant take cover, but he should be where the direction of the wind will help him. Take the dog to the starting point you have chosen, the line attached to the dog's collar, sit with the dog on your left, and make quite sure that neither you nor anything else will be likely to obstruct, particularly any object around the vicinity of the 'suspect'. Then pat the dog and continue patting for about a minute (this is very important as on future occasions the dog will associate these actions with an intended 'seek'). Now point in the direction you wish the animal to go—just slightly to the left or right of the assistant, depending on which way the wind will help the dog—and release the dog with the command 'Seek, seek'.

The handler should remain where he is, but if it is obvious that the dog is going wrong, he should walk slowly towards the 'suspect', if necessary guiding the dog by pointing in the direction required, and repeating the command 'Seek'. The dog, on discovering the assistant, should be immediately rewarded by the assistant.

Pointing helps to teach a dog the direction in which it is required to work, but much practice is required before a dog becomes proficient by this method. The handler should, as is customary with sheep-dogs, eventually be able to point with either hand to guide the dog when it is necessary and if he is in a position to do so.

These exercises should be performed three times each day, increasing the distance on each occasion, and on different sites.

As soon as the dog gives you confidence that he will always return to you on being called to hand, allow him to seek freely with a short line about two feet long attached to the collar and, eventually, without a line at all, and when you are sure he understands the word 'seek' practise the same procedure in a disused building or other premises. The dog each time he finds his 'suspect' should be rewarded by that person.

The short line, referred to above, is substituted for the long line because the latter tends to hinder the dog, as will be discovered when the dog is 'seeking' on its own. The short line permits the handler to control his dog at the beginning of the exercise, when he is getting the animal to sit by his side prior to directing him to 'Seek'. It is also long enough for the handler to hold the dog, should he expect the dog to 'point' before he 'seeks' his quarry. To the question, 'Why not use the lead instead of the short line?', may I remind the reader that I have already referred to the ring attached to the end of the lead and the danger of the dog being hurt by it and being completely put off any exercise.

After the sixth or seventh time the dog 'seeks' in his preliminary training, encourage the dog to 'speak' on discovering his quarry. This is most important and, if necessary, the animal should be encouraged by the assistant to do so, either by offering the dog food if he 'speaks' or, later, by using a thin stick on the legs to make him bark, care being taken that the stick is made use of only sparingly, otherwise the dog may be put off his work if he receives only the stick for all his efforts. Waving the hand up and down may be all that is necessary on the part of the quarry to make the dog bark.

In any case, for a considerable period the dog should be rewarded each time he finds his 'suspect' on his own, and even on refresher courses it is a good policy occasionally to feed the dog for his efforts.

When the dog has thoroughly understood the above, take him to a quiet country road, on the long line, and ask several assistants, each carrying a thin switch, to hide. Again the direction of the wind should be noted and the dog not allowed to see the assistants while they are hiding themselves. Walk with the dog as before, very slowly, in the centre of the road, and let the dog find each person in turn. Make sure that the dog 'speaks' to each person as he discovers him. Here the application of a thin switch may help the dog to 'speak'. After perfection on a quiet road, practise the same exercise at night, and later in a street where there are other people. Occasionally, let one of the assistants lie down motionless as though dead; but he must get up immediately the dog barks, and reward the animal.

The object of these exercises is to ensure that the dog always gives tongue at anything strange or suspicious so that the attention of the handler is immediately attracted. This applies particularly when patrolling premises, whether the dog has been directed to seek or not.

Take the dog into a building, and on the command 'Seek', release him and let him search the premises until the handler is satisfied that either the quarry has been found or that no one is there. Bear in mind that the dog should find a 'quarry' as often as possible, for if he continually fails to find a quarry he may lose the desire for this type of work. Many occasions will arise when no one is present, but whenever the handler is sure someone is present, such as on a refresher course, or on seeing someone enter those premises, then the dog must be allowed to find that person.

Searching premises is a most important part of a dog's work and if it is obvious, on being asked to 'seek', that he is getting 'stale', it is advisable to start all over again. This sometimes happens after almost a month's training on the course, in which event it is advisable to starve the dog for a day or so, or reduce his rations to half his normal daily feed. Note that the dog at this time is fed only when on seeking exercises, and then only when the handler is satisfied that he has performed his work satisfactorily. Generally, it will be found that dogs who go 'stale' and who are re-trained like this make excellent dogs for searching premises.

Provided the dog has received a well-regulated course of discipline in his first month of training it should now no longer be necessary to reward him during the obedience exercises.

The following exercise can be done as an extension of 'stopping' a person, as so often happens when a 'suspect' has run off and disappeared down a street or behind buildings and the dog has to search for the criminal before being able to 'stop him'. Or, again, it can be employed for dogs that are reluctant to 'seek' but very good at 'stopping' a person.

The dog should see a 'suspect', wearing a protective sleeve, about a hundred yards away, run off and disappear behind a wall or building. The 'suspect' should try to confuse the dog by hiding some distance away from where the dog saw him disappear, say some twenty-five yards away, so that the dog must of necessity 'seek' for him. After holding the dog back for a minute or two the handler should release the dog, and he may have to do so just before the assistant disappears. On the next run, the handler should keep hold of the dog for several minutes before releasing him, to allow the assistant plenty of time to select a good hiding place. On the run following that, he should hold the dog back still longer, each time making it a little more difficult for the dog. Don't forget that immediately the 'suspect' is discovered, the animal is fed by the 'suspect'.

On these occasions the protective sleeve is an added incentive to the dog to make him 'seek'. Eventually, feeding the dog is dispensed with, the 'suspect' runs off from his hiding place just before the dog finds him, and is stopped by the animal. When the dog has got accustomed to stopping the quarry in this way he is then made to bark at the quarry on finding him, and the quarry should make off, and again be stopped by the dog.

Sometimes, in order to keep the dog barking, he is given small pieces of meat by the 'suspect' until the handler arrives. The 'suspect' is then escorted back, and can try to make a getaway.

When searching large areas, such as a field or park land, at night, with practically no wind, if any, to help the dog, it is best to circle the area, with the dog on the lead, and to work in smaller and smaller circles towards the centre. In this way the handler can be sure that he has covered the whole area, whereas if he sends the dog off on its own, the dog may or may not find the 'quarry'. By circling the area the chances are that time will be saved by knowing how much of the ground has been covered. If the dog 'points' during this procedure the handler will be able either to release his dog or approach any person or persons quietly and, possibly, without himself being seen, and thus be able to observe their movements, see what they are doing, and act accordingly.

It will have been noted that the dog has to earn his food during most of the exercises already explained, and this is especially important in the 'seeking' exercises, because the dog will become used to barking at his quarry when he finds him, in the belief that he will be rewarded for his efforts. Any tendency to want to bite or molest his quarry is thus obviated. Some schools training dogs for searching premises believe that if the dog is first taught to do man-work on a padded suit, the dog can subsequently be taught to search premises by allowing a 'quarry' to run off in the sight of the dog, the dog automatically 'cottoning on' to searching premises. The chances are that if the dog is so trained he will form the habit of biting his 'quarry' when he gets up to him.

It is better to teach the dog, in the period of time it takes to teach the dog man-work, to search for his quarry so that he learns during this period not to molest anyone in a stationary position whether hiding or not, and to draw the attention of his handler by giving tongue.

Some people only require a dog that will search premises, and they do not want man-work included in the training because they are incapable of coping with a dog so trained. It is essential, therefore, that training a dog to search premises should be taught on the lines of this section of the book.

'TRACK'
This is the command given by a handler when he wishes his dog to find a suspected criminal, or other person, or object, by 'ground scent'.

Teaching a dog to track is very difficult in the early stages, but once the animal has become proficient at tracking it becomes a most interesting and fascinating part of the handler's work, the dog's ability at times seeming to border on the uncanny. Before dogs were introduced to this type of work, well-meaning people, including the police, in trying to discover in which direction a felon had gone cast about in every direction except, as a rule, the right one. With a tracking dog, however, there is always a fair chance that wasted effort will be reduced to an absolute minimum. On several occasions when I was able to arrive with my dog at the beginning of a search of premises from which suspects had made a getaway, police officers in cars waited for a lead from the dog to see in which direction the suspects had gone before themselves setting off. On one occasion it was a railway station closed down for the night, and there the suspects were found. This was team work. It was of no importance who made the arrest so long as the suspects were caught, and the dog, having supplied the first clue, played a constructive part in the arrest, though, of course, it would have been more satisfying to me, the handler, had the dog been given the opportunity to track the suspects down on his own.

Only about 5 per cent of a person's scent is left on the ground when he or she travels over that ground. It is the gas formed by disturbing the ground that the dog follows, inter-mingled with that small amount of scent left by that person. For instance, grass or other foliage when walked over becomes bruised and immediately emits a gas. The harder the ground, the more difficult it is for the dog to track over, and newly laid tarmac is hopeless.

It takes about two years to make a good tracking dog, but that does not mean the dog will do no useful work during that period. It does mean, however, that before the dog is likely to be really efficient, that period will almost certainly be necessary, since he will have to work in so many varying conditions, such as the weather and the time of day. Night time is more favourable than the day, and a slightly damp atmosphere helps, although rain can wash all scent away. The period that elapses before arriving at the scene of a crime also plays an important part, for it is said that a track is cold after two hours. For these reasons, in the early training for tracking, circumstances that are as favourable as possible for the dog should be chosen. He should also be given every opportunity to use his olfactory organs to their best advantage. Never smoke a cigarette or permit others to do so in the proximity of a dog that is about to go on a 'seek' or 'track'; and a dog that is kept indoors will probably take some twenty to thirty minutes to acclimatise its olfactory organs to atmospheric conditions. A dog uses his nose as number one sense, his ears next, and his eyes last.

Every stage in teaching a dog to 'track' should be well thought out before it is started. Some dogs, of course, learn quicker than others, and not all dogs will 'track' or ever become reliable at it, but it is always a help when searching premises, even to dogs who will never become expert trackers.

Dogs trained for this type of work should never be allowed to chase or be used for game. The game instinct must be discouraged and eliminated as far as possible if a dog is to be at all proficient in tracking a human being. This is another point in favour of the Alsatian, which readily adapts itself to man-work.

The first exercises in tracking must be short, and should be conducted in wooded country where the ground is flat and covered with soft earth or leaf mould. Make quite sure that no one has walked over the ground during that day, then ask your assistant, who should carry at least three pieces of meat in a tin, to make a track about twenty yards long in a straight line. He should begin by leaving a piece of cloth, about the size of a lady's handkerchief, on the ground at his starting point, and the cloth should have been on his person for some hours before dropping it on the ground. (Generally, I keep a piece of cloth in my pocket for these occasions.) With one foot dragging along the ground, to make a visual track for the benefit of the handler and dog, the assistant should then walk for a convenient distance to the nearest tree, say some twenty yards away, behind which he can conceal himself. In the meantime, the dog, which must not be allowed to see the assistant make the track, is with the handler behind another tree or bush. The handler should observe the assistant make off and note the position he has taken up.

No time lapse should be allowed in the early stages, the dog quickly arriving at the place where the cloth has been left. The visual track should be casually noted by the handler as soon as he approaches, so that he can guide the dog. The handler now gets the dog to lie down, with its nose on the cloth, on the left of the handler, both facing the track. Holding the dog by the collar with the left hand, together with the lead, the handler then bends down, holds the cloth flat in his right hand, forms it into a cup, places it over the dog's nose, and holds it there for several seconds. (Try to count ten.) Pointing to the visual track with the right hand, and retaining the cloth in the same hand, the handler releases his hold on the dog's collar, but keeps hold of the lead several inches from the collar, and with the command 'Track', 'Track', uttered slowly and at about every other pace in the initial stages (later he will use the command only once), he walks gently forward along the track. At the same time he must make the dog keep its nose near the ground, doing this as best as he can with the left hand. Bending down and guiding the dog is very exhausting to the handler, but it is absolutely necessary in these early stages if the dog is to understand what is required of it.

At first the dog will probably try to wander off the visual track, but it must not be allowed to do so. If, however, it is clear that the lesson must begin again because, possibly, both dog and handler have wandered off the track, re-start at that part of the track that has been completed successfully. *Do not go back to the beginning* because the handler's scent will have been added to the track and the dog will become confused and wander off again. As soon as the dog discovers or comes upon the assistant he should immediately be rewarded with one piece of meat.

Have two more similar tracks made by the assistant, shortly after each other, complete, and finish tracking exercises for that day.

Next morning let the tracking exercises be completed first; in fact, let it be the first exercise of any morning, while the dog is fresh and there is less likelihood that anybody else has walked over the ground. Use different ground each day, and begin about a hundred yards away from the ground that was practised on on the previous day.

The assistant goes off again leaving the cloth behind him, taking a few pieces of meat with him. This time he should drag his foot for some thirty yards, hide behind a bush or tree, but the visual track need not be in a straight line as on the previous occasion; it can be in the form of a semicircle. The handler and dog come up to the start of the track, as before, and complete the track. Two similar tracks are made and completed by the dog, one piece of meat being given by the assistant to the dog on each occasion the dog finds him. The total time taken at this stage is about three-quarters of an hour.

Three tracks are made each day for about two weeks, based on those already described. The distance, however, should be increased slightly each day until, after two weeks, the dog is able to complete a track of about a hundred yards, each track having varied in pattern. The visual part of the track can gradually be dispensed with, depending on the progress made. Sometimes it takes about three weeks to get a dog to track without any visual track to assist it. The long line should take the place of the lead as soon as the handler feels that he no longer needs to remind the dog to keep its nose to the ground. It will take some time for the handler to get accustomed to using the line to the best advantage, for the amount he lets out will depend entirely on him. Generally, he shortens the line if he has to help the dog, and lets it out when the dog starts to quicken its pace or there are no obstacles in the way of the track. A dog may suddenly turn back on a track, and it is then the handler will need to have about half the line out to take a sudden jerk on the hands. Be careful to let the line out slowly because a keen dog will draw the line quickly through the hands and it may blister the skin.

The three tracks a day can now be reduced to two a day for a few days, but each track should be made slightly longer, and after that only one track a day is done.

The above are the preliminary exercises for tracking, and once proficiency in them has been achieved tracking proper can begin.

Ask the assistant once again to leave the cloth at a starting point and, without leaving a visual track, to walk off in any direction he chooses for some two to three hundred yards across country into some small hills or such like, and hide himself. Allow about ten minutes for the assistant to complete the track, take the dog to the beginning of the track, make the animal lie down as before, and get him on the move until he completes the track. Each time he is successful he should be rewarded, and from now onwards he should do one track a day varying the details as in the following examples.

The next track is taken over a small stream, or over hills and such like for a distance of about 500 yards. Similar tracks are made, still over foliage, but crossing small paths at right angles only, until the dog has been learning to track for about six weeks. Make sure that the dog completes each exercise successfully, otherwise the track should not be lengthened. If he should keep failing to find his 'quarry' reduce the one track to two half tracks a day until he can do them well and with ease.

Next start on grass that after about a hundred yards leads on to about twenty yards of gravel, then over grass or other

'*Stop him*'. The dog takes hold of the protected arm and swings the 'criminal' round and round to make him dizzy and confused, so that he cannot strike or kick the dog.

The early stages of teaching a dog to give tongue on discovering suspected criminals hidden in grounds, woodland, etc. The assistants gradually increase the area to be searched. A small stick helps to encourage the dog's keenness. The dog should give tongue to each person he finds.

Keystone Press

The dog acts, without any word of command, as soon as his handler is knocked down, thereby being taught to protect his master at all times.

The dog goes to the assistance of his handler immediately the 'criminal' tries to get away. This assistance is of paramount importance should the 'criminal' attempt to injure the handler. No word of command could be given if the handler was being strangled.

foliage for about forty yards, then over gravel again for about another twenty yards, and so on until he can track over gravel or paths with very little foliage to assist him.

Most of these tracks should be done without the wind assisting the dog; that is, the wind should be blowing from where the dog begins his track and towards the quarry. Occasionally, try to arrange the track so that at some point when he has nearly completed it the wind will be blowing in his favour, just to let him make use of his 'seeking' instincts. After all, the object of teaching a dog to 'track' and 'seek' is so that he will find his quarry as soon as possible.

Another good variation in tracking is for the assistant to climb up a tree on to a wall. This is to make the dog look up when he comes to hideouts such as are likely to be used by a criminal. Also, allow the dog to track to a small building, the door of which is then opened by the handler so that the dog can 'seek' those premises.

After about four weeks' training small articles such as gloves may be found *en route*, but the handler should pick up such articles rather than allow the dog to do so, because experience has proved that a dog that is expected to pick up articles on a track and give them to the handler becomes disinclined to continue tracking. It is done in competition work, when the type of article that is to be found is known and unlikely to harm the dog, but in practice it should not be done. If the article is bulky it should be left, or hidden, or its position noted so that it can be collected later; any attempt to carry will probably mean that that is the end of the track, simply because you will be unable to continue without impeding the dog.

There are other important reasons why a dog should be taught only to indicate where an article is lying and not pick it up. If it is a revolver, gun, or other weapon fingerprints will be of exceeding importance, and the dog's saliva together with his teeth gripping such articles can obliterate vital evi-

G

dence, apart from the fact that such weapons may go off. Razor blades, knives, and sharp instruments can also be dangerous.

My views on the subject of discouraging a dog from picking up articles on a track may be criticised, particularly as, earlier, I have included lessons on teaching a dog to 'fetch' articles, which seems paradoxical. Like so many things in training a dog there will always be contradictions, and the circumstances must be the guide. The methods I have described are derived from my own personal experiences; others may deduce their own methods and meet the complications that ensue in their own way.

To continue, occasionally allow the dog to chase an assistant who has been found and tries to run for it; he should, of course, be wearing a protective sleeve. Generally, in these circumstances the handler lets the line go because he will lose vital seconds if he tries to take the line from the dog's collar, and he may have to wind all the line in to do so, by which time the culprit will have escaped. Take the line off only if the dog is likely to be impeded in its pursuit of the 'quarry'. Only a very good dog will chase such a person the first few times after he has tracked and found a quarry, since tracking is one of the most exhausting exercises he is called on to do. Nevertheless, it should be tried, since in some circumstances it may prove useful. Incidentally, the handler himself will be pretty well winded, especially as on most tracks he will have been running to assist and encourage the dog.

Now practise tracks that do not include articles left *en route* but, say, only a footprint. Then, later, cast about and try to let the dog pick up a track, by which time the handler should have learnt much himself in the art of picking up a track to help the dog. After a while do the same sort of thing from a building window, with soft earth outside, then from hard ground.

Don't expect a dog to track one person, then almost immediately track some other person. It takes about an hour for a trained dog to be able to change from one person's scent to another. In other words it takes that amount of time for the scent of the first person to be eliminated from the dog's nose. With some dogs it takes longer, so don't blame the dog if he is not always successful in tracking a second person, or shows little interest.

To be able to track a person who has slept in a bed in a detention cell, escaped and made his way, say, to a railway station some two to three miles away, is the apex of tracking, and it will take about two years to train a dog to this proficiency, and only then if the dog has been given the opportunity of doing some form of tracking every day.

I well remember a case which, I believe, has never been excelled before or since by a tracking dog. A colleague of mine and his dog Shaun were called to a smash-and-grab at a jeweller's shop in Whitton High Street an hour or so after midnight. Two velvet ring trays and their contents had been taken. The handler and dog were taken by car to the scene of the crime, and the dog, taking the scent from the half-brick used to break the window of the shop, picked up a track that led his handler to Kingston Bridge, other police following in a car. Under Kingston Bridge the dog found one empty tray. Continuing to track, the dog next led the police along the Thames riverside, into Bushy Park, and out again on to the riverside, where, stopping at the water's edge, the second empty tray was found. The dog then intimated that it wanted to cross the water. A boat lying close by was used to convey dog and handler to the other side of the river. Shaun again picked up the track, which led the police to the closed gates of Hampton Court Railway Station. The dog was lifted over the gates, and then took his handler to a railway carriage at the far end of the station platform. Two men were found asleep in one of the compartments, and subsequently they were arrested. The distance of the track was approximately four miles.

GUARDING AN OBJECT, CAR OR PREMISES

Begin by tying the dog to an outside wall or shed, where the handler can see the dog without himself being seen by the animal, and only about a yard or so away from the dog. In other words the dog is tied to the wall, and the handler is round the corner.

The dog is directed to lie down as far as the lead from the wall, which is tied at ground level, will permit. The handler places an article belonging to himself on the ground within a foot or so from the dog, and just out of his reach; something about the size of a handkerchief will do to start with. The handler should strongly impress on the dog, by drawing its attention to the article he is about to leave and touching it several times, that he wants the article guarded, adding 'Watch, watch'.

The handler then takes up his position by the side of the wall or shed and tries to avoid the dog's seeing him. He keeps a strict eye on the dog, which must stay in the down position. To keep the dog in the down position the handler should have a supply of pebbles to throw at the dog's rump every time the animal attempts to get up, at the same time, of course, using the command 'Down'.

An assistant should provide himself with a thin stick which, unless he has to use it, he keeps in his hand on the far side from the dog as he passes him. The dog should not see the stick unless it is necessary for the assistant to use it. The assistant now begins walking to and fro past the dog, about twenty paces before he gets to him and twenty paces beyond him, walking, of course, parallel with the wall, and he should bend down slightly and attempt, and only attempt, to take the article. Never take the article away in the initial stages; not until the dog becomes aware of what can happen, and it may take several days before the dog begins to understand. If the dog makes no attempt to warn off the assistant, by barking or snarling at him, then the assistant should raise the stick and threaten to strike the dog. (It will seldom be necessary to apply the stick to the dog's legs if the animal has previously been taught to 'speak' correctly; the raising of the stick should be all that is necessary.) If the dog barks or snarls the assistant should jump quickly to one side, as though frightened off by the dog, and proceed to hurry away. This action by the assistant will generally encourage the dog to bark, and help teach the animal what is required. The handler then quickly appears and makes a fuss of the dog, saying 'Good boy' and so on.

It may occasionally be necessary for the assistant to use the stick on the dog's legs, and when he has to do this to make the dog bark he should use the words of command 'Speak', 'Watch', 'Watch him' and, on the dog responding, he should immediately jump to one side. As the dog becomes proficient at this exercise the handler can increase his distance from the dog watching his possessions, and take longer to return to the dog to praise him.

When it seems that the dog has become aware of the activities of one assistant, introduce another assistant; then employ two assistants walking in opposite directions. Then introduce several assistants, and instruct only one to attempt to take the object lying on the ground. Then ask two or more, approaching from opposite directions to try to take the object. At this stage one of the assistants should wear a protective sleeve and actually take the article, the dog being permitted to hold him until the arrival of his handler.

It should be appreciated, of course, that only three attempts a day should be practised in teaching the dog to 'watch' an article, and it may take a week or so to perfect. Also, as in other exercises, it is wise to choose different places for the exercise.

Having taught the dog thus far, you can now teach him to guard a car or, better still, a small van. Tie the dog inside the vehicle using as much line as possible, but in such a way that the dog cannot get at the hand of an assistant who will be expected to place his hand inside the car or van. Care should also be taken to see that the dog is not likely to injure his feet or nose when the assistant closes the door. The handler then leaves the vehicle, and hides himself behind a tree or other convenient spot, out of sight of the dog, but where he can see the animal. After a few minutes an assistant, who tries to keep out of sight of the dog, approaches the vehicle, gently opens one of the doors, and attempts to hit the dog with a stick, with only just sufficient force that will make the dog bark or snarl. The assistant, who should likewise encourage the dog to bark, closes the door as hastily as possible and makes off. Have another assistant do the same on any other door of the vehicle. Then both assistants should act together, until the dog begins to realise that he must be on the look-out for all intruders when his handler is away.

The handler should return to the vehicle after each attempt has been made by an assistant to molest his vehicle, and praise his dog as quickly as possible.

The next procedure is for the assistant to try to take a small object from inside the car, which again should be left just beyond the reach of the dog, and placed on the front seat by the handler, who directs the dog to 'watch' the article. The procedure is much the same as when leaving an article on the ground for the dog to 'watch'. The handler then walks off and hides some twenty yards away. After a minute or so the assistant, who has previously armed himself with a protective sleeve, slowly approaches the vehicle from the opposite direction and, doing his best to avoid being seen by the dog, opens one of the doors and attempts to take the article. The dog is permitted to hold him by the protective sleeve, the assistant immediately yelling out as though hurt, and trying to struggle with the dog until the arrival of the handler.

After the dog has been trained to protect in this way, should the handler have a friend with him the handler should take care that he, *not* his friend, enters the vehicle first, and directs the dog accordingly.

Leaving a dog to guard premises can be achieved by similar methods as described in the previous paragraphs.

Tie the dog with the lead to a hook suitably placed a few yards inside the entrance hall to the premises. The dog should be in the down position. Say to the dog, 'Watch', and leave the premises by the front entrance. The door should be left ajar, the handler hiding in a suitable place, say near a window, where he can see the dog and the animal cannot see him. An assistant, again provided with a stick, enters and raises his stick as if to strike the dog; if the dog barks he makes a hasty retreat almost slamming the door behind him. Should the dog fail to bark, then the stick is used on the dog's legs, but only with sufficient force to make the animal bark and go for him. The handler on each occasion praises the dog when it has done the right thing. From now onwards the handler approaches the dog from the entrance opposite to the one the assistant has left, in other words from the front or rear of the premises as the case may be.

Introduce another assistant who will enter the premises from the rear as the first assistant leaves by the front; he also strikes out at the dog if the animal fails to respond. This will make the dog watch the premises from all entrances and inform his handler, by barking, that an intruder has entered.

A room in which to tie the dog up can now be chosen, and an assistant is told to try to enter it by an open window, the same procedure being gone through.

When the handler is satisfied that his dog will bark at an approaching intruder on the practice premises, let an assistant have a protected sleeve on the right arm and a stick in his left hand and quietly make entry. This time the dog should be off the lead, and as the animal attempts to go for him, he immediately presents the protected arm to the dog. The handler will, of course, enter the premises, order the dog off, and praise him. Practise for about two weeks, sometimes at night, then occasionally in order to keep the dog up to scratch.

WATER RESCUE WORK

The words of command most applicable in this kind of work are 'Fetch', 'Leave', 'Hand', and 'Down'.

Handlers whose sphere of work lies in the vicinity of rivers, lakes, and reservoirs where it is possible they may come across someone who is in danger of drowning, due either to accident or by design, need to know how to train their patrol dogs to play an effective part in bringing the casualty to land.

Clearly, if a dog is to effect a rescue in deep water, the first essential is that it should be able to swim. It will surprise many people to learn that not all dogs can swim, and that some do not even like water. Many dogs are like human beings, they have to be taught to swim.

The second essential is that the dog should have learnt to retrieve, both in and out of water. If the dog has been taught to retrieve on land, as explained under the heading 'Fetch', p. 41, that lesson now needs to be extended to include retrieval across or in water.

Choose fine days to practise this type of work so that the dog can easily dry himself with the minimum of effort. Ascertain if he can swim by throwing a piece of wood into calm water, and asking him to fetch. Throw it only a short distance, just far enough to encourage him to go into the water. If he enters readily, and retrieves the piece of wood, repeat the process twice more at slightly longer distances, and finish training for the day. Do three retrieves each day for a whole week until you are satisfied that the dog is quite at home in water.

If it is found impossible to induce the dog to enter the water on his own, the handler should choose a pond or an expanse of water that will allow him to get facing the dog with water between them, attach the long line to his collar, and order the dog to go down at the water's edge. Now walk round to the opposite side of the pond, call the dog, and pull on the long line. If the expanse of water is a stream, the handler may have to go to the opposite bank to practise this, or throw the line to an assistant stationed there, and get him to draw the dog over the water. The dog's name and word of command 'Hand' should be used repeatedly when trying to induce the dog to swim towards the man pulling on the line. It is a promising sign if the dog re-enters the water and swims back to the handler on his own, when encouraged to do so. The handler should try to induce the dog to enter the water from the opposite side of the river, after it has previously been taken there by an assistant. But until the handler is sure the dog will always enter the water and swim towards him in as direct a line as possible, the line should always be available for the assistant to pull the animal back, or prevent the dog from making for the footbridge or route taken by the assistant to get to the opposite bank, and spoil the exercise.

As before, the swimming lessons should be given only three times a day for about a week, until the dog jumps into the water of its own accord and enjoys swimming for its own sake. Next, repeat the stick-throwing exercise, but this time throw large sticks into the water and get the dog to retrieve them by using the command 'Fetch'.

When satisfied that the dog can swim well, and only then, the rescue work proper can begin. First, improvise a dummy, by attaching two pieces of two-inch by two-inch wood, about three feet long, together, in the form of a cross, making sure the cross-pieces are firmly tied. Cover this frame with an old coat or jacket, or sacking will do, by wrapping it round tightly. Attach a loop of rope to the dummy so that it can be easily clipped to the long line. Now throw the dummy into the water, only a few yards from the bank, and command the dog 'Fetch'. It will help the dog if the handler gently draws the dummy back towards him as soon as the dog has got a grip on some part of the dummy with his mouth. Try to avoid getting the dog's legs entangled in the line, otherwise he may be put off wanting to continue with the exercise. As the dog gains proficiency, and when it is felt he can be relied on to bring the dummy to land, attach the line to his collar, throw the dummy in the water, and direct the dog to fetch. This time as soon as the dog takes a hold on the dummy he should be drawn gently towards the handler. Again, practise only three times a day for about a week.

It will now be necessary to make a larger dummy, one that is as like a body as possible. Again, the dummy is thrown into the water, short distances at first, and the dog directed to retrieve it on the command 'Fetch'. Each time the dog enters the water have the line attached to his collar so that he can be assisted in bringing the dummy to land. Early experience will have accustomed the dog to being impeded by the line occasionally, but avoid this happening as much as possible. Make quite sure that the dog does not savage the dummy, once he has landed it, and practise artificial respiration on the dummy, ordering the dog to stay in the down position while so doing. This will get him used to the procedure. Occasionally, the handler should step into the water and take hold of the dummy, at the same time ordering the dog to go down or leave. The dog *must* loosen his hold on the dummy immediately he is directed to do so.

Now take the dog to that part of the water where it is

possible for an assistant to hide; for example, behind a bank, in long grass, or behind a wall. The dog should be with the handler some twenty yards away and should at no time be permitted to see the assistant. The assistant should now throw the dummy into the water, quickly conceal himself again, and then shout loudly, 'Help', repeating the cry several times. The dog, on the line, is quickly brought to the scene and directed to fetch the dummy. If possible, get the dog to jump into the water from a low jetty or bank, or even over a low obstacle that will enable him to shorten the distance, and therefore the time in which he will eventually be able to rescue a person. The dog, assisted by the handler pulling on the line, then retrieves the dummy. Practise for several days, until the dog becomes familiar with the procedure and also the words likely to be used by a person in difficulty in water.

The next step requires an assistant to enter the water with his arms protected in some way, by wearing the protective sleeve to start with, then with something like sacking, and permitting the dog to take hold of his arm and drag him back to the water's edge. The handler then takes over and goes through the procedure of artificial respiration, etc., whenever possible.

It will be appreciated that the handler who has to patrol near water and who is likely to use his dog for rescue work must always carry with him sufficient line, with trigger-clip attached, ready for use on all occasions. The line for attaching to the dog's collar is an essential, for in dangerous waters, or with a struggling man, the dog may become exhausted, unable to continue his work, and have to be brought back to land quickly for its own safety. The line may also serve a useful purpose if the person to be rescued is able to hold on to it, when both rescued and rescuer can be brought back to safety. It may also be possible to use the line on its own, by throwing it out to the person in difficulties.

An early opportunity should be given to the security trained dog which has been taught to swim to swim a small stream in order to stop and hold a suspect. The handler should, of course, choose a place where he can easily cross the water without getting wet himself—for instance near a bridge.

The method is generally as follows: the 'suspect' goes to the other side of the water, wearing a protective sleeve, and stands close to the water's edge at least twenty yards from a bridge. The dog—previously kept out of sight—is then brought on to the scene opposite the 'suspect' and quite close to the water; the 'suspect' waves his arms, shouts, if necessary, to attract the dog, and splashes the water with a stick as though he has just come out of it. The dog is then released with the command 'Stop him'. The procedure is then as for an ordinary chase and the detaining of a suspect. Next, practise with the 'suspect' having gone some twenty yards inland, and the dog released twenty-odd yards before coming to the water on the opposite bank.

TEACHING A DOG TO REFUSE FOOD

This should be the last lesson a dog is taught, and then only when the handler is satisfied that his dog is well-enough trained in every other aspect. It may be necessary, occasionally, to allow a dog to take meat from an assistant, when, say, the dog is having a refresher course, especially on a seek, if the dog has not had an opportunity to practise this work for some time.

The method is as follows. Stand with the dog on your left side on the lead and have an assistant about two yards in front of you and the dog. The assistant has a stick in his right hand, concealed behind him, and offers the dog a piece of meat in his left hand. As the dog moves towards the assistant's left hand, to take the meat, the assistant hits the dog on his legs as hard as is necessary to prevent the dog taking the meat. After practising several times it will be noticed that the dog is no longer eager to take the offered meat. He may bark instead, which is all to the good and should be encouraged, as this tends to deter people offering food.

Practise for several days, changing the assistant during different times of the day, and in ever-changing places.

Next, get several assistants standing in a line to offer, in turn, meat to the dog, each one using his stick, when necessary, to prevent the animal taking the food.

After this exercise place the dog in the down position on grass land, the end of the lead being pegged into the ground. (Avoid placing meat on gravel, stony or sandy ground, because if the dog should by chance grab the meat he may take a stone with it into his stomach.) Get the assistant to drop a piece of meat just out of reach of the dog but close enough to him to tempt the dog to snatch at it. If the dog moves forward towards the meat, the assistant hits him with his stick on the legs and rump, again only with as much force as is necessary to stop the animal getting the meat. The meat is then picked up by the handler, who has been in the vicinity all the time, and placed in a tin, which he leaves some three or four yards away. This meat is never given to that particular dog; it may, however, be given to others, as part of their diet.

The same exercise is repeated with two or three assistants, each dropping meat within easy reach of the animal and preventing the dog from getting it by the use of a stick, if necessary. The lesson needs to be practised as often as possible, for a considerable number of days and in a variety of places, if it is to have effective results.

Finally, the dog should be tied up and left with a large piece of meat literally to look at for several minutes by one of the assistants, and if at any time it shows any signs of attempting to take the meat it should be promptly rebuffed with a stick or catapult, used on his rump.

A word of caution: *never use a catapult if a dog is looking direct at you*, and always use it on the side or rear of the animal. If you do use a catapult when a dog is looking at you or in your direction, you may hit his eyes or teeth and you will never forgive yourself. A catapult should be used only by a person experienced with such a weapon (*see also* p. 53).

Teaching a dog to refuse food is only effective if the animal is not really hungry. In other words, a dog that has been starved for a week or so will forget all about food refusal; it may be cautious, but eventually it will succumb because of hunger if some person offers it food. The only effective way to prevent a dog eating food that has been poisoned and thrown to it by someone wishing it harm is to muzzle the dog.

BAD HABITS AND THEIR CORRECTION

Most bad habits in a dog have been contracted because his owner has not taken the trouble to correct the dog at the proper time. They can be corrected but, of course, the longer the habits have been permitted to go on, and the older the dog is, the more difficult they are to eradicate.

The average dog-owner is convinced he is capable of training his dog, but in fact very few can, generally because they have not the slightest idea how to do it. Some say they could do it if they had the time, but the truth is that if dog-owners would take the trouble in the first instance to acquire the necessary knowledge, and to devote a little patience and time to it, they would save themselves a considerable amount of worry and have a dog that is a pleasure to themselves and not a nuisance to others.

Attending dog-training classes is a great help, but even here their activities are limited, and whereas the average dog-owner will find such courses beneficial, the dog that is just a little more than disobedient is always a difficult proposition. Most classes hesitate to take dogs that fight, or dogs that are difficult with strangers, etc. With such it is wiser to obtain the services of a professional trainer. It is possible for an owner to correct his dog, but it must be realised that all dogs cannot be dealt with in the same way, and the professional who has far wider experience with all types of dogs is more likely to get good results, especially with the larger breeds. Even so, no professional dog trainer can give a guarantee that his efforts will be successful, any more than the best teacher in the world can guarantee that a child will get through his or her eleven-plus examination.

The dog will, however, be considerably improved, and provided the owner is willing to continue training in accorddance with the instructions given by the professional trainer a degree of satisfaction can be attained. Once the basic training has been instilled into the dog then it is only a matter of going daily through all the exercises in obedience, which should take only about thirty minutes each morning, for the next month or so, and occasionally afterwards. This will enable the dog to get used to the articulation of the owner.

Up to the time of writing I have trained some 600 dogs since leaving the police force, an average of about four dogs a month. About 30 per cent have been trained for security work alone—the others mostly for obedience.

It may be said that relatively few people are capable of controlling and working a dog that has been trained by a professional. If that were true I would soon be out of business and, what is more to the point, many dogs would have had to be put to sleep if they had not received some proper form of training in obedience. It is essential that the professional trainer should, as I do, give instructions to a client to enable him to carry on where he, the professional, leaves off. This includes the method used in training the particular dog. Judging by the number of dog-owners who have written to me to state how pleased they are, and the repeat orders I receive, I am more than convinced that a dog professionally trained is generally worth while. I have, of course, one advantage over many professional trainers of security dogs in that I have had practical experience of dealing with criminals, and with a dog as a partner.

Correcting the Dog that Fights with Other Dogs
Put the muzzle on the dog, and his chain collar with the long line attached. Take the dog to a tree that has a strong root, about two inches in diameter, protruding from the ground surface. Scrape the earth from under the surface root, pass the line under the root, and pull the line through as far as it will go. Since the dog is attached to the line he will be obliged to lie down and must remain there as long as the person who is holding the line keeps it taut. Care, however, should be taken that the dog is not held down too long or too tightly. 'Down' is the word of command.

It is now necessary to introduce another dog and handler, who, taking great care to see that his dog does not bite the dog that is lying down, sits his dog on the tethered animal for a few minutes, and then takes him off again. The handler holding the tethered animal now releases that dog for a few minutes, and the procedure is begun all over again. The next step is to introduce other dogs, each of which, in turn, is made to sit on the offender for a few minutes. Next, each dog should be directed, in turn, to jump over the dog that is lying down, if necessary the handler of each dog pulling his dog over the offender. Then try to sit two dogs on him; then a dog sitting on him and another jumping over them both. If this is done in an organised manner, it will take about a week to achieve success, practising about twenty minutes daily.

At the end of the week, leave the muzzle off the offending animal, but retain the chain collar with line attached, and, to make sure the dog is not likely to get out of hand, continue

'*Watch him*'. In the initial stages encourage the dog occasionally by letting him get hold of the assistant by the protected arm.

Incite the dog to bark loudly at people who refuse to depart, thus encouraging him to disperse a hostile crowd.

'*Seek*'. Lead the dog with the wind coming from the assistant. As soon as the dog points in the assistant's direction, encourage the animal to go up to him . . .

. . . The dog should be rewarded on approaching the assistant.

to use the root of the tree to hold him down, so that if by chance the dog should get up it is quite easy to draw him to the ground again. Go through the same procedure with a leather collar instead of the chain collar. After about a fortnight it should be possible to make a dog sit on the offender for several minutes without any attachments other than the lead and leather collar. Walk round both dogs saying, 'Down', 'Down', 'Stay'.

Sometimes an owner has two dogs that persist in fighting with each other, and up to the time of correcting them it has been necessary to keep both dogs apart in the house, and when exercising them outdoors.

The procedure is practically the same, but in this case the owner needs no second person to assist him, provided both dogs have been trained individually to have become obedient enough during the exercises described in the earlier sections devoted to the training of stay and down positions. As both dogs, however, cannot be trusted with each other, it will be necessary to muzzle them both, and they must be made to lie down within a foot of each other's noses. To do this, use an iron pin at the end of each of their leads, the leads, of course, being fully stretched for this purpose. Provided both pins are well placed in the ground there is no possibility of either dog getting free. The dogs are now directed to down, and stay, the commands being repeated several times if necessary. Walk over each dog swinging another lead or a conveniently looped rope, and bang a stick on an old tin or pail to make as much noise as possible near the dogs. Every now and then throw the tins over both dogs, the object being to distract the attention of them both.

Then, if neither shows any inclination to get up, unmuzzle one dog, and take it round to the back of the other dog, but do not allow any attempt on the part of the dog that is lying down to get up and attack the dog walking behind it. The

H

owner, of course, is always in a position to withdraw the dog he has hold of, and the iron pin would, if necessary, prevent the other dog attempting to get near the dog being handled. The owner should now reverse the procedure: muzzle the dog he was handling first, peg it down, remove the muzzle from the other dog, and pass up and down behind the dog he first handled.

Having practised daily for some twenty minutes on each occasion for about a week, the procedure becomes familiar to both dogs, and the handler can now practise jumping one dog over the other, but the handler must always see that he does this from the rear of the animal being jumped over, so that he is always in a good position to withdraw the dog he is handling. At the end of two weeks it should be possible to follow the previous instructions without muzzles on either dog, and he can practise making one dog sit on the other as it passes over the back of the one lying down, again only from the rear of that dog, until both dogs are familiar with the procedure.

During this period both dogs should be encouraged to walk with each other, with muzzles on, round the premises of the owner, and if it is possible, they should sometimes be handled by a stranger while they are being exercised. Even if the stranger can handle only one dog, and the owner the other, it will help both dogs to become accustomed to each other. Then only one dog—the more aggressive—need be muzzled, and later neither.

As it is necessary that the owner should be able to leave both dogs together without having to worry about them fighting with each other, in the initial stages both dogs should be tied, in the down position, for several minutes, and the time increased until they can be left together for several hours, the owner appearing on the scene at intervals, according to the progress made.

Hand-shy Dogs

Nervous dogs often try to evade people who try to touch them and will do almost anything to keep away from strangers. Often, they will snap at people wishing to make their acquaintance, a state of affairs that has probably come about through someone hurting them in puppyhood. Much patience is required on the owner's part to get the dog over this nervousness. It could have been caused by a youth touching the dog with a stick or other weapon when the animal was being exercised in the main street, and the owner may have much difficulty in getting the dog to pass this type of person.

The remedy is to introduce the dog to as many people as possible, and it must be handled in and out of doors by different people whenever it is convenient to do so. The dog may have to be muzzled in the early stages, and held by the owner, to enable other people who understand the position to pat or stroke the animal.

In all probability the dog will struggle, and may even attempt to bite through the muzzle, and it is on these occasions that the owner must try to sooth the animal and not be deterred from encouraging other people to make the dog's acquaintance.

As soon as it is apparent that the dog no longer minds being handled by some person other than the owner, then ask that person to feed the dog, through the muzzle at first, then, if the dog appears content to take the food this way and does not resent that person, without the muzzle. The lead, however, must be held by the owner. It may take a few days to get as far as this. The person concerned should, in the first instance, place the food on a flat piece of wood or other convenient article so that he is not likely to have his fingers bitten. Then, if all goes well, he can feed the dog with a piece of meat held in the centre of the flat hand. This routine is then continued for a month or so with different people, all of whom should be made aware of the objects, and have sympathetic natures.

It will be appreciated that the dog should always be given his daily ration by someone other than the owner, thereby expediting the correction of the dog.

After a little while it should be possible to take the dog into a street frequented by a few people, then into main streets, and in and out of shops. The dog must get accustomed to people passing by and obstructing its path, so that later, when it is taken into crowded parts, it behaves rationally. It may take time to achieve this object but it will certainly be well worth the effort.

The owner must also try to understand that, in all probability, he himself has been responsible for the dog's becoming nervous, by not taking the dog out and about when he first acquired him. It is, therefore, up to him (or her) to try to remedy the trouble. The excuse that the dog is too big or too difficult to handle is a poor one. Enquiries regarding the possible growth of the animal should have been made when the animal was obtained. In any case now is the opportunity to treat the dog in the correct manner, and to help the dog overcome hand-shyness, by training him in obedience.

Dogs Jumping Up at People

This habit can be a nuisance and an embarrassment to the owner, especially when ladies are present. Such boisterousness is likely to spoil clothes, ladder stockings, and so on and is generally due to over-excitement on the part of the dog, who wants to be taken notice of immediately, which is natural with normal young dogs who really only want to play. This bad habit must be corrected as early as possible because someone may get hurt. With the puppy, it is easy. All that is necessary is a sharp smack on the puppy's side, which will knock him down, and the word 'No' uttered emphatically. With a larger dog the remedy has to be more forceful, and it must, of course, be done by the handler in the first instance. The action is to bring the knee up sharply into the animal's chest every time he jumps up in front of him, and at the same time forbid the dog with the word 'No'. It should always be done when the dog is least expecting the rebuff. If the dog should whine or become temporarily winded, so much the better; he will understand all the more quickly that he is not to jump up.

Dogs Worrying Sheep or Cattle

For those living in country districts a dog that worries farm stock can cause no end of trouble, and may entail fines or the destruction of the dog. The only sensible thing to do is to keep the dog on the lead when in a district where sheep or other animals are known to be, thus preventing the dog worrying any farm animal that might appear suddenly on the scene. Dogs that live in such places should not be fed on mutton.

Most dogs, however, can be cured of this habit by the following methods, which must of necessity be ruthless.

Take the dog to a field where sheep are enclosed, and where, if the dog should accidently get loose, he cannot get at the sheep before you can get him back quickly. Put the chain, choke collar on the dog with the long line attached, both of which must be very strong indeed and not likely to break. If necessary have two such collars and lines attached, both lines being of similar length.

The dog, in all probability, will be struggling to get at the sheep, so, taking a strong hold of the end of the line (or lines), let the dog go. As he is nearing the end of the line on his run towards the sheep, anticipate when he will get to the end of it and give an extra hard pull on the rope. To be effective this must be done at the same time that he is stopped by the rope. In other words let the dog jerk his neck, and as hard as possible. Repeat this three times in the course of a day. If after the second day the dog does not hesitate before chasing the sheep then employ a spiked collar and go through the same procedure, and let him fall head over heels so that he cannot possibly forget it. If necessary, wear gloves to take the strain on the line.

When you feel satisfied the dog will not attack sheep grazing behind an enclosed fence, take him to a place where several sheep are grazing in the open, but be sure that you are capable of stopping him getting at the sheep, by means of the collar and line as already practised. The command 'Down' should be used as soon as the dog starts to run towards the sheep, so that he will understand, if by chance on future occasions he should get loose, that the command 'Down' is generally followed by a pain in his neck that stops him in his tracks.

Dogs Going for Chickens or Other Domestic Pets
This can be overcome by constructing a box strong enough to prevent the dog biting his way out and large enough to allow him to turn round in with ease. The open end of the box should be barred either with very strong wire netting or iron bars. The side has a door to enable the dog to be put into the box or taken out, and the roof is protected with felting, as a precaution against rain.

Place the open end of the box against the chicken-run wall within view of the chickens and put the offending dog inside his temporary kennel. Leave him there for several days, taking him out for exercise three times a day, for an hour on each occasion, and feed and water him during these periods. He will soon get used to seeing chickens and will leave them alone.

A wire cage large enough to contain the dog placed inside the run may be a little ambitious, but the effect is quicker, especially if the chickens should be cockerels of about twelve months or older. Unfortunately these cages are expensive, but it may be possible to borrow one. Care, of course, must be taken in placing the dog in and taking him out of the cage so that he does not accidently get among the chickens. With the wooden-box kennel placed outside the run there is no possibility of his getting loose, and even if he does, there is still the wire netting of the chicken run to prevent his disturbing the birds.

For dogs that go for cats, place both the dog and the cat in separate boxes, then put both boxes together at about an angle of forty-five degrees to each other. Leave the animals together every night for about a week, or as long as is found necessary. The boxes are constructed as described above, to enable both animals to see each other without being able to get at each other.

3

Dog/Handler Relationship

ONLY the handler should work his dog, and he should be the only one to look after the animal's welfare. If it is necessary for someone else to look after a dog whose handler is sick, or away for some other reason, strict instructions should be given that the dog is to be exercised on the lead only, for half an hour in the morning and half an hour in the evening, and that in a quiet place. No attempt should ever be made by those left to look after dogs to try to work them.

Firms, factories, estates, and so on, apart from having their dogs insured, for obvious reasons, should note that before organising dog patrols they should make quite sure they are in a position to:

    (*a*) provide transport whenever necessary;

    (*b*) assist in any legal proceedings, and encourage handlers to take offenders to court if necessary.

If handlers are not backed up when they carry out their work efficiently they soon become discouraged and apathetic. Nothing disheartens them more than being given the impression that they are only there for moral effect. Some people employ untrained handlers with this object in view, and while this may be all right up to a point, an occasion may arise when their bluff will be called, and evidence that dog and handler were properly trained will be required.

Only then will it be realised how important correct training is in order to maintain moral effect, and genuine security.

Firms and factories often ask if it is necessary to teach a dog to 'track' when their premises are not very extensive, and suggest that the cost and time taken in training a dog for security work could be curtailed. I generally enquire if the dog will ever be called upon to search such premises, and if the answer is 'yes', explain that seeking and tracking are tied up together, and that tracking develops the dog's nose for 'seeking' or searching premises. It will be observed that a dog taught to track often puts his nose to the ground in a 'seek' if he cannot scent the criminal by direct scent. This tuition therefore greatly assists the dog in locating his quarry in the quickest possible time, and those extra minutes may prove vital in preventing a criminal escaping. I believe in teaching a dog as much as it can learn, thereby enhancing the value of the dog's abilities. Refresher courses of at least one day a month should be arranged, as a dog taught any type of nose work can lose this faculty if not given regular opportunities for using it.

The practice of sending a dog into premises and directing him to 'seek' unnecessarily is to be deprecated because he will soon lose the desire to find anyone, and begin to idle his time away. At least every other time he is searching premises he should be given the opportunity of finding someone, an assistant if necessary. It is rather like learning shorthand or a language; without practice one soon forgets what one has learned. A good handler will see that his dog is given every opportunity, in the correct manner, to search premises and thus keep his dog up to scratch.

Sometimes I have been asked by firms and local authorities if I would select handlers from a number of volunteers who have applied for the job. In most cases I have declined, simply because I do not think this is a responsibility one should accept without knowing the background of the applicants. Nevertheless I have interviewed several men and have selected those who seemed capable of handling dogs, a week or so prior to training, and forwarded my observations to the authority concerned.

Generally, I decline to recommend too young a person with little worldly knowledge, or a too old or incapacitated person who could hardly be expected to cope with intruders. I try to sum up their reasons for wanting to become a dog handler, and note any initiative or keenness they may have for this type of work. I ask them if they have ever been in trouble, which would prevent them becoming bonded by an insurance company; whether they have been in many jobs before, so that I can get an idea of the likelihood of this job being just a passing phase that would not justify the expense and time involved in the training; their idea of what to expect of a trained dog; and if they have accommodation to kennel a dog, and facilities for transport if it is not provided by the employer. I also make enquiries regarding their hobbies, family life, and so on, so that I can ascertain if they would be suitable for working on an estate, council or factory site. This is important, since they may have certain preferences for working in town or country.

At the beginning of the training, all trainees are given course cards (about the size of a postcard) on which the words of command are inscribed. An explanation regarding the use of these words and as much detailed information as possible is given at the same time.

It is a strange fact that most dogs of European origin dislike people from other continents, and considerable caution should be exercised when non-Europeans are in the vicinity since complaints may result if this advice is ignored. It may take quite a while for a dog to accept a non-European handler.

WORDS OF COMMAND

Name of dog first " "

HAND	to come
SIT	
SPEAK	
HEEL	to heel on the left
RIGHT	to heel on the right
DOWN	
DEAD	
STAND	
FETCH	
CARRY	
STAY	in position required
UP	to jump
NO	to correct
KENNEL	to go to
QUIET	
AWAY	to go on its own

Extra commands for security dogs

WATCH HIM	to bark at a person
STOP HIM	to chase and hold a person
SEEK	to seek for a person
TRACK	to track a person
FEEDING	**12 noon. Biscuits, butter, sugar, milk.**
	6 p.m. or after a tour of duty $1\frac{1}{2}$ lb. RAW meat.

Fast on Sundays. Water always available

Training Classes

A dog should be handled by one person only. The welfare of a multi-handled dog is always in jeopardy, for no personal interest is taken in a dog that is shared by two or more people, and if the dog is sick, the last person to handle the animal is bound to say, 'Well, the dog was all right when I saw him last', and all the more emphatically if the animal is nearly dead. A dog is quite unable to work for or obey more than one handler, hence a multi-handled dog can be a danger to all. Even the family pet has genuine affection for only one person in a household, and obeys implicity only that one.

The ideal training class comprises four dogs and four handlers. They should, if possibly, begin and end the training course together. A class of this size is easy to manage and its members work well one with another. They are able to pair off each day for 'seeks', 'tracks', etc., without becoming too familiar with the dogs, and in obedience training in particular a class of this size will be found just right for giving demonstrations and conducting tests. It will also be found that each dog gets the correct amount of training each day, whereas in a larger class some exercise is almost certain to be neglected. If the four handlers have the good fortune to be employed by the same firm or authority, nothing could be better, since all duties can be made to fit in, including holidays and sickness, when one member's dog can be cared for by another member.

In training, competition and enterprise very soon become apparent, and four dogs with their handlers inevitably create this atmosphere, as well as a spirit of sportsmanship. I have noticed that the comradeship so built up during this period seems to last for many years both with the dogs and the handlers, lady handlers included.

Men trained with dogs think twice before giving up their employment, generally on account of the dog. If they do decide to leave, they invariably ask if they may keep the animal, in which case it will depend on whether or not the dog can be transferred to another employee.

If it does become necessary to transfer a dog to another handler because the former handler has left, the correct procedure is to have the dog retrained *together with the new handler* under the supervision of the trainer, as the new handler may know nothing about training.

This takes about a month, if the dog's previous training was based on the principles laid down in this book. Even then, only about 50 per cent of dogs will transfer in that period—and much depends on the new handler.

Buying a 'Trained' Dog

Be very careful of purchasing dogs that are advertised as trained, especially guard dogs or those required for security work. A dog cannot be very well trained if it will just go to any person; certainly no dog that is worth its salt will do so. However, if you are tempted, insist on having the dog examined by your own veterinary surgeon, not that of the person selling the dog. This will mean that the dog must be with you a few days, because the temperature of a dog always goes up when transferred from one owner to another, which means that it will be a day or two before you can take the animal to the 'vet', and during this period you can ascertain whether the dog will suit you. In other words, you have the dog on trial for a few days. If this procedure is not followed the advertised dog, described as trained, may not like his new owner or the owner the dog, and useless expense will have been entailed.

Those people who desire a security dog and have little or no idea how to acquire or train such a dog should employ the services of a professional security dog trainer and get him to obtain a suitable dog of about ten to twelve months old. The owner should attend during the whole of the training course.

It is no good attending occasionally, as this will only upset the dog; it must be every day or not at all. It should be realised that the person the dog has to protect should be present and that he himself must be trained to use the dog, and form a team spirit between person and dog. It is worth while to enquire from either your local veterinary surgeon, the Kennel Club, the R.S.P.C.A., or the police for the names of trainers they can recommend.

Alternatively, and as a second best, if the owner cannot possibly attend the training course the dog should be kept by the owner for two to three months, during which period the dog will get to know the new owner, and he or she the dog. After this the dog can be sent to the trainer for the prescribed training period and, when it is handed back to the owner, the dog should very quickly recognise him or her.

Collars and Chains
All kennel chains not in use should be hung on a peg provided for that purpose. If the swivel is left on the ground the dog may tread on it and get it caught in one of his feet. Should this happen, immediately obtain the assistance of several people to hold the animal down, while a hacksaw is brought into use to cut the swivel, and free the dog's foot. A muzzle may also have to be used on the dog to prevent its biting one of the helpers.

A leather lead should be as long as a handler is tall, and never less than four feet by one and a quarter inches wide and a quarter-inch thick. Leads should be oiled occasionally with a good leather oil, which preserves the leather. Leather leads can be made from old reins or leather belts, if difficulty is experienced in obtaining new leads. As leather stretches, use the thin end of the leather for the handle of the lead, and attach the thick part to the swivel. The thin part will become even thinner after use. A two-inch steel ring running free in the loop of the lead can be put to many useful purposes, but particularly for tying on to railings. The leads can be joined together, or the lead can be used as a truncheon by connecting ring and swivel together (*see* photograph of equipment required for training).

Avoid chain leads with small leather handles. As a rule they are short in length, it is possible to use only one hand with them, and invariably the hand gets damaged. Also, it is impossible to control a dog with such a lead. If the dog has been allowed to bite his lead, then have a short chain attached to a long leather lead, and try to correct the bad habit the dog has got into.

Leather collars should be twenty-six inches long by one and a quarter inches wide by quarter-inch thick, the 'D' being placed at one end, and the buckle immediately after the 'D'. This is exactly the reverse order to that of collars as usually sold in shops. The leather of a collar so made will last considerably longer and will be found safer to use because in the normal collar the 'D' is the first thing to come off, especially those used with dogs who come in contact with water. If the 'D' should break through the leather on the collar recommended, it will still be attached to the rest of the collar. The owner's name and address should always be inscribed on it. (This type of collar can be made up at any good saddler's.)

Food

Meat is the main diet for a dog, and it should be half fat and half lean. The fat helps to keep down hysteria. Ordinary butcher's meat such as cheek of bullock, shin of beef, or breast of mutton is best. See that chilled meat is always warmed. Milk, and a piece of butter the size of a walnut, should be given daily, the butter supplying any vitamins the dog may lack. (Don't fool yourself with margarine.) Horseflesh contains no fat, and should not be given. Biscuits are of little use, although they tend to please those dogs who will eat them. They should never serve as the main meal, being composed only of flour and water.

Never give bones. They stick in the anus and cause trouble to a dog trying to pass motions. Don't be hoodwinked into the common belief that the animal has worms if he is seen drawing himself along on his bottom. This is not so. If the dog continues in this action, the obstruction, invariably caused by bones, must be removed. A dog's teeth will last longer if *not* given bones.

Avoid giving tinned food. Meat from a tin has been known to contain that part of a beast that has received a vaccine. After having eaten from one tin, one dog went into a coma, causing considerable distress to its owner who thought the dog might not survive. No human being would like to live permanently on tinned food, nor would a dog, but unfortunately a dog has no option but to eat what it is given. Tinned food may be a handy and convenient way of buying and storing animal foods but it is neither satisfying nor good for the welfare of the dog.

A dog is a carnivorous animal, and vegetables are of little use to him. He has no cheeks to help him chew, and is only able to tear up meat into a convenient size so that he can swallow it. The juices in his stomach act as his teeth and masticate the food. These juices cannot break down the walls of a vegetable, and if they could there would be no allotments left standing for miles around. The only vegetables he can eat are those that have passed through another animal, such as a horse, cow or a rabbit. His eagerness to eat them when they are offered in that form is only too apparent. If nature had intended his food to be cooked before he ate it, she would have attached a little gas stove to his hindquarters.

Never feed a dog prior to a journey. Let it fast for twenty-four hours before a journey, and *never muzzle a dog after a meal,*

'*Track*'. Make the dog lie down in front of the object left by an assistant and allow the dog to scent it for several seconds.

Keep the dog's nose on the visual track, pointing to the ground; the object left by the assistant should be folded into the palm of the hand.

Allow the dog to continue on the track as far as he can, then, if necessary, encourage him by pointing towards the ground.

Teaching a dog to guard his handler's belongings.

Bad habits. Correcting dogs that fight with each other. Each is made to sit on the other and so they become friendly.

especially if he has to make a journey. He cannot get rid of any food if he is sick, and will surely suffocate.

Grooming

A dog should be groomed every day. Train the dog to put his front feet on a low chair or box kept especially for the purpose of grooming. A dog soon forms the habit of standing in this convenient position the moment he observes brush and comb in his master's hand. Hold the dog by the collar with the left hand, and with the right holding the comb, first comb the coat against the grain, then with the grain. The object of grooming the animal against the grain first is to loosen any old hair. Follow the same procedure with the brush. Don't forget to remove the collar occasionally as parasites get lodgement there, and a dog cannot get rid of them while the collar is on. A chamois leather is excellent for drying a dog, especially after he has been exposed to wet weather. It should be kept for this purpose only.

Kennels

A healthy dog needs plenty of fresh air, and should, therefore, be kept outside in a well-constructed and warm kennel, where, in spring and autumn, he will moult. If he is kept indoors he will moult all the year round.

Kennels (Fig. 3) should be constructed of wood and built in sections. The kennel should be at least four feet six inches wide by four feet deep. It should stand clear of the ground by nine inches; its height at the front, from ground to roof, should be four feet three inches and at the back three feet nine inches. The clearance under the floor of the kennel allows for cleaning, and normal falls of snow in Britain seldom amount to a foot in depth. The timber used for the sides should be tongued and grooved, and that for the roof and floor should not be less than one inch thick or it will warp. The flat roof, which

I

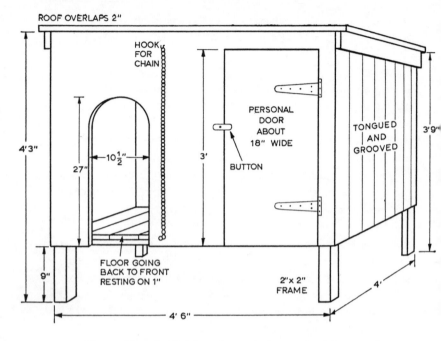

ROOF OVERLAPS 2"

HOOK
FOR
CHAIN

4'3"

27"

10½"

PERSONAL
DOOR
ABOUT
18" WIDE

BUTTON

3'

TONGUED
AND
GROOVED

3'9"

9"

FLOOR GOING
BACK TO FRONT
RESTING ON 1"

2"x 2"
FRAME

4'

4' 6"

Fig. 3. Kennel. Floorboards are loose so that they can be turned over in wet weather; wood for floor and roof is 1 inch thick.

slopes from front to back and overruns the frame, should be made so that it will slide off. At the front of the kennel, besides the dog's entrance, there should be a personal door, about eighteen inches wide and three feet high for easy access. The inside of the kennel should be periodically creosoted, and outside it should be painted. Inside, also, a partition one foot high should be arranged in grooves so that it can be lifted out. Its purpose is to enable plenty of hay or straw to be put there in winter months, for warmth, and so that it can be removed in hot weather when neither hay nor straw will be necessary.

A sack provides a useful blind over the entrance to the kennel, which should be lowered at night time in bad weather.

In such accommodation the dog provides its own heat, and is perfectly comfortable. If a chain is required, then it should be six feet long, and as thick as possible, so that it cannot become a danger to the legs of the dog. A pail of water, changed daily, should always be available at the side of the kennel, and, if necessary, tied to the kennel to prevent its falling over.

This type of kennel is ideally suited for countries that have similar climates to Britain where conditions necessitate the dog's sleeping almost in a hay-box, in which it generates its own heat to keep warm in winter. In hot countries, however, this form of kennelling is entirely unsuitable, as the animal must be kept as cool as possible and well protected from the sun's rays, especially when the dog is resting during the hottest hours of the day. Everything possible should be done to prevent the dog suffering from heat exhaustion or from being disturbed by flies and other insects. The kennel must therefore be erected on a cool site, well shaded from the sun and as spacious as possible. The wearing of collars and chaining up must be avoided while the dog is off duty and so housed. The kennel will have to be built with an outside run covered with very close wire mesh, and it may have to be reinforced with iron bars placed at convenient intervals, or thicker wire mesh. Both the kennel itself and the run outside should be at least seven to eight feet high, the sleeping quarters about ten feet by six feet, and the outside run about ten feet by twelve feet. There should be an easy and convenient wooden platform for the dog to lie on, about one foot from the ground, and two personal doors, one made for easy access from the inside and the other from the outside.

Puppyhood and 'Old Age'
Except for house training, no dog should be taught obedience until it is six months old. Prior to that age it should be taken out as often as possible, especially after meals, to allow it to

wander on grass. The herbs in the grass induce the dog to perform its natural functions, and when he is turning round several times he is following his ancestral habit of making a convenient spot for himself, by pushing the long grass down.

At eight years of age a dog has reached the end of his working life; after that, he needs an arm-chair. For that reason it is best to obtain a dog at about twelve months old to get the full value out of his training.

As a final observation, never boast about your dog's activities. Let him make his own reputation, and remember that with the best-trained dog in the world it is the handler, or the man behind the gun, that counts. The dog will do only as much as the handler wants him to.

Appendix

A.K.C. OBEDIENCE REGULATIONS*

Effective January 1, 1969

Purpose

Obedience trials are a sport and all participants should be guided by the principles of good sportsmanship both in and outside of the ring. The purpose of obedience trials is to demonstrate the usefulness of the pure-bred dog as a companion of man, not merely the dog's ability to follow specified routines in the obedience ring. While all contestants in a class are required to perform the same exercises in substantially the same way so that the relative quality of the various performances may be compared and scored, the basic objective of obedience trials is to produce dogs that have been trained and conditioned always to behave in the home, in public places, and in the presence of other dogs, in a manner that will reflect credit on the sport of obedience. The performances of dog and handler in the ring must be accurate and correct and must conform to the requirements of these regulations. However, it is also essential that the dog demonstrate willingness and enjoyment of its work, and smoothness and naturalness on the part of the handler are to be preferred to a performance based on military precision and peremptory commands.

* Reprinted by permission of the American Kennel Club.

CHAPTER I

General Regulations

SECTION 1   *Obedience Clubs*   An obedience club that meets all the requirements of The American Kennel Club and wishes to hold an Obedience Trial at which qualifying scores toward an obedience title may be awarded, must make application to The American Kennel Club on the form provided for permission to hold such trial. Such a trial, if approved, may be held either in conjunction with a dog show or as a separate event. If the club is not a member of The American Kennel Club it shall pay a license fee for the privilege of holding such trial, the amount of which shall be determined by the Board of Directors of The American Kennel Club. If the club fails to hold its trial at the time and place which have been approved, the amount of the license fee paid will be returned.

SECTION 2   *Dog Show and Specialty Clubs*   A dog show club may be granted permission to hold a licensed or member obedience trial at its dog show, and a specialty club may also be granted permission to hold a licensed or member obedience trial if, in the opinion of the Board of Directors of The American Kennel Club, such clubs are qualified to do so.

SECTION 3   *Obedience Classes*   A licensed or member obedience trial need not include all of the regular obedience classes defined in this chapter, but a club will be approved to hold Open classes only if it also holds Novice classes, and a club will be approved to hold a Utility class only if it also holds Novice and Open classes. A specialty club which has been approved to hold a licensed or member obedience trial, if qualified in the opinion of the Board of Directors of The American Kennel Club, or an obedience club which has been approved to hold a licensed or member obedience trial may, subject to the approval of The American Kennel Club, offer additional non-regular classes for dogs not less than six months of age, provided a clear and complete description of the eligibility requirements and performance requirements for each such class appears in the premium list. Pre-Novice classes will not be approved at licensed or member obedience trials.

SECTION 4 *Tracking Tests* A club that has been approved to hold licensed or member obedience trials and that meets the requirements of The American Kennel Club, may also make application to hold a Tracking Test. A club may not hold a tracking test on the same day as its show or obedience trial, but the tracking test may be announced in the premium list for the show or trial, and the tracking test entries may be included in the show or obedience trial catalog. If the entries are not listed in the catalog for the show or obedience trial, the club must provide, at the tracking test, several copies of a sheet, which may be typewritten, giving all the information that would be contained in the catalog for each entered dog. If the tracking test is to be held within 7 days of the obedience trial the entries must be sent to the same person designated to receive the obedience trial entries, and the same closing date should apply. If the tracking test is not to be held within 7 days of the obedience trial the club may name someone else in the premium list to receive the tracking test entries, and may specify a different closing date for entries at least 7 days before the tracking test.

The presence of a veterinarian shall not be required at a tracking test.

SECTION 5 *Obedience Trial Committee* If an obedience trial is held by an obedience club, an Obedience Trial Committee must be appointed by the club, and this committee shall exercise all the authority vested in a dog show's Bench Show Committee. If an obedience club holds its obedience trial in conjunction with a dog show, then the Obedience Trial Committee shall have sole jurisdiction only over those dogs entered in the obedience trial and their handlers and owners; provided, however, that if any dog is entered in both obedience and breed classes, then the Obedience Trial Committee shall have jurisdiction over such dog, its owner, and its handler, only in matters pertaining to the Obedience Regulations, and the Bench Show Committee shall have jurisdiction over such dog, its owner and handler, in all other matters.

When an obedience trial is to be held in conjunction with a dog show by the club which has been granted permission to hold the show, the club's Bench Show Committee shall include one person designated as 'Obedience Chairman'. At such event the Bench Show Committee of the show-giving club shall have sole jurisdiction over all matters which may properly come before it, regardless of whether the matter has to do with the dog show or with the obedience trial.

SECTION 6 *Sanctioned Matches* A club may hold an Obedience Match by obtaining the sanction of The American Kennel Club. Sanctioned obedience matches shall be governed by such regulations as may be adopted by the Board of Directors of The American Kennel Club. Scores awarded at such matches will not be entered in the records of The American Kennel Club nor count towards an obedience title.

All of these Obedience Regulations shall also apply to sanctioned matches except for those sections in which it is specified that the provisions apply to licensed or member trials, and except where specifically stated otherwise in the Regulations for Sanctioned Matches.

SECTION 7 *American Kennel Club Sanction* American Kennel Club sanction must be obtained by any club that holds American Kennel Club obedience trials, for any type of match for which it solicits or accepts entries from non-members.

SECTION 8 *Dog Show Rules* All the Dog Show Rules, where applicable, shall govern the conducting of obedience trials and tracking tests, and shall apply to all persons and dogs participating in them except as these Obedience Regulations may provide otherwise.

SECTION 9 *Immediate Family* As used in this chapter, 'immediate family' means husband, wife, father, mother, son, daughter, brother, or sister.

SECTION 10 *Pure-Bred Dogs Only* As used in these regulations the word 'dog' refers to either sex but only to dogs that are pure-bred of a breed eligible for registration in The American Kennel Club stud book or for entry in the Miscellaneous Class at American Kennel Club dog shows, as only such dogs may compete in obedience trials, tracking tests, or sanctioned matches. A judge must report to The American Kennel Club after the trial or tracking test any dog shown under him which in his opinion appears not to be pure-bred.

SECTION 11   *Unregistered Dogs*   Chapter 16, Section 1 of the Dog
Show Rules shall apply to entries in licensed or member obedience
trials and tracking tests, except that an eligible unregistered dog
for which an ILP number has been issued by The American Kennel
Club may be entered indefinitely in such events provided the ILP
number is shown on each entry form.

SECTION 12   *Dogs That May Not Compete*   No dog belonging
wholly or in part to a judge or to a Show or Obedience Trial
Secretary, Superintendent, or veterinarian, or to any person of
such person's immediate family or household, shall be entered in
any dog show, obedience trial, or tracking test at which such person
officiates or is scheduled to officiate. This applies to both obedience
and dog show judges when an obedience trial is held in conjunction
with a dog show. However, a tracking test shall be considered a
separate event for the purpose of this section.

No dog shall be entered or shown under a judge at an obedience
trial or tracking test if the dog has been owned, sold, held under
lease, handled in the ring, boarded, or has been regularly trained
or instructed, within one year prior to the date of the obedience
trial or tracking test, by the judge or by any member of his immediate family or household, and no such dog shall be eligible to compete. 'Trained or instructed' applies equally to judges who train
professionally or as amateurs, and to judges who train individual
dogs or who train or instruct dogs in classes with or through their
handlers.

SECTION 13   *When Titles Are Won*   Where any of the following
sections of the regulations excludes from a particular obedience
class dogs that have won a particular obedience title, eligibility to
enter that class shall be determined as follows: a dog may continue
to be shown in such a class after its handler has been notified by
three different judges that it has received three qualifying scores for
such title, but may not be entered or shown in such a class in any
obedience trial of which the closing date for entries occurs after
the owner has received official notification from The American
Kennel Club that the dog has won the particular obedience title.

Where any of the following sections of the regulations requires
that a dog shall have won a particular obedience title before competing in a particular obedience class, a dog may not be shown in

such class at any obedience trial before the owner has received official notification from The American Kennel Club that the dog has won the required title.

SECTION 14 *Disqualification* A dog that is blind or deaf or that has been changed in appearance by artificial means (except for such changes as are customarily approved for its breed) may not compete in any obedience trial or tracking test and must be disqualified. Blind means having useful vision in neither eye. Deaf means without useful hearing.

A dog that is lame may not compete at any obedience trial and must be disqualified unless an official veterinarian, after examining the dog at the judge's request, certifies that the lameness is due to a temporary condition. Lameness means any derangement of the function of locomotion. Even when the veterinarian certifies that the lameness is due to a temporary condition, the dog shall be excused by the judge if, in the opinion of the veterinarian, competition would be injurious to the dog.

If a judge has evidence of any of these conditions in any dog he is judging at an obedience trial he must, before proceeding with the judging, notify the Superintendent or Show or Trial Secretary and must call an official veterinarian to examine the dog in the ring and to give the judge an advisory opinion in writing on the condition of the dog. Only after he has seen the opinion of the veterinarian in writing shall the judge render his own decision and record it in the judge's book, marking the dog disqualified and stating the reason if he determines that disqualification is required under this section. The judge's decision is final and need not necessarily agree with the veterinarian's opinion except in the case of lameness to the extent specified above. The written opinion of the veterinarian shall in all cases be forwarded to The American Kennel Club by the Superintendent or Show or Trial Secretary.

The judge must disqualify any dog that attempts to attack any person in the ring. He may excuse a dog that attacks another dog or that appears dangerous to other dogs in the ring. He shall mark the dog disqualified or excused and state the reason in his judge's book, and shall give the Superintendent or Show or Trial Secretary a brief report of the dog's actions which shall be submitted to AKC with the report of the show or trial.

When a dog has been disqualified under this section as being blind or deaf or lame or as having been changed in appearance by artificial means or for having attempted to attack a person in the ring, all awards made to the dog at the trial shall be cancelled by The American Kennel Club and the dog may not again compete unless and until, following application by the owner to The American Kennel Club, the owner has received official notification from The American Kennel Club that the dog's eligibility has been reinstated.

Spayed bitches, castrated dogs, monorchid or cryptorchid males, and dogs that have faults which would disqualify them under the standards for their breeds, may compete in obedience trials if otherwise eligible under these regulations.

No dog shall be eligible to compete if it appears to have been dyed or colored in any way or if the coat shows evidence of chalk or powder, or if the dog has anything attached to it whether for medical or corrective purposes, for protection, for adornment or for any other reason, except for certain breeds to the extent only that they are normally shown in the breed ring with the hair over the eyes tied back. The judge, at his sole discretion, may agree to judge such a dog at a later time if the offending condition has been corrected.

An obedience judge is not required to be familiar with the breed standards nor to scrutinize each dog as in dog show judging, but shall be alert for conditions which may require disqualification or exclusion under this section.

SECTION 15 *Disturbances* Bitches in season are not permitted to compete. The judge of an obedience trial or tracking test must remove from competition any bitch in season, any dog which its handler cannot control, any handler who interferes willfully with another competitor or his dog, and any handler who abuses his dog in the ring, and may excuse from competition any dog which he considers unfit to compete, or any bitch which appears so attractive to males as to be a disturbing element. In case of doubt an official veterinarian shall be called to give his opinion. If a dog or handler is expelled or excused by a judge, the reason shall be stated in the judge's book or in a separate report.

SECTION 16 *Novice A Class* The Novice A class shall be for dogs not less than six months of age that have not won the title

C.D. No person who has previously handled a dog that has won a C.D. title in the obedience ring at a licensed or member trial, and no person who has regularly trained such a dog, may enter or handle a dog in this class. Each dog in the class must have a separate handler, who must be its owner or a member of the owner's immediate family. The same person must handle each dog in all exercises.

SECTION 17 *Novice B Class* The Novice B class shall be for dogs not less than six months of age that have not won the title C.D. Dogs in this class may be handled by the owner or any other person. A person may handle more than one dog in this class, but each dog must have a separate handler for the Long Sit and Long Down exercises when judged in the same group. No dog may be entered in both Novice A and Novice B classes at any one trial.

SECTION 18 *Novice Exercises and Scores* The exercises and maximum scores in the Novice classes are:

1. Heel on Leash	35 points
2. Stand for Examination	30 points
3. Heel Free	45 points
4. Recall	30 points
5. Long Sit	30 points
6. Long Down	30 points
Maximum Total Score	200 points

SECTION 19 *C.D. Title* The American Kennel Club will issue a Companion Dog certificate for each registered dog, and will permit the use of the letters 'C.D.' after the name of each dog that has been certified by three different judges to have received scores of more than 50 per cent of the available points in each of the six exercises and final scores of 170 or more points in Novice classes at three licensed or member obedience trials, provided the sum total of dogs that actually competed in the regular Novice classes at each trial is not less than six.

SECTION 20 *Open A Class* The Open A class shall be for dogs that have won the C.D. title but have not won the title C.D.X.

Obedience judges and licensed handlers may not enter or handle dogs in this class. Each dog must be handled by its owner or by a member of his immediate family. Owners may enter more than one dog in this class but the same person who handled each dog in the first five exercises must handle the same dog in the Long Sit and Long Down exercises, except that if a person has handled more than one dog in the first five exercises he must have an additional handler, who must be the owner or a member of his immediate family, for each additional dog, when more than one dog he has handled in the first five exercises is judged in the same group for the Long Sit and Long down.

SECTION 21 *Open B Class* The Open B class will be for dogs that have won the title C.D. or C.D.X. A dog may continue to compete in this class after it has won the title U.D. Dogs in this class may be handled by the owner or any other person. Owners may enter more than one dog in this class but the same person who handled each dog in the first five exercises must handle each dog in the Long Sit and Long Down exercises, except that if a person has handled more than one dog in the first five exercises he must have an additional handler for each additional dog, when more than one dog that he has handled in the first five exercises is judged in the same group for the Long Sit and Long Down. No dog may be entered in both Open A and Open B classes at any one trial.

SECTION 22 *Open Exercises and Scores* The exercises and maximum scores in the Open classes are:

1. Heel Free	40 points
2. Drop on Recall	30 points
3. Retrieve on Flat	25 points
4. Retrieve over High Jump	35 points
5. Broad Jump	20 points
6. Long Sit	25 points
7. Long Down	25 points
Maximum Total Score	200 points

SECTION 23 *C.D.X. Title* The American Kennel Club will issue a Companion Dog Excellent certificate for each registered dog, and will permit the use of the letters 'C.D.X.' after the name

of each dog that has been certified by three different judges of obedience trials to have received scores of more than 50 per cent of the available points in each of the seven exercises and final scores of 170 or more points in Open classes at three licensed or member obedience trials, provided the sum total of dogs that actually competed in the regular Open classes at each trial is not less than six.

SECTION 24 *Utility Class* The Utility class shall be for dogs that have won the title C.D.X. Dogs that have won the title U.D. may continue to compete in this class. Dogs in this class may be handled by the owner or any other person. Owners may enter more than one dog in this class, but each dog must have a separate handler for the Group Examination when judged in the same group.

SECTION 25 *Division of Utility Class* A club may choose to divide the Utility class into Utility A and Utility B classes, provided such division is approved by The American Kennel Club and is announced in the premium list. When this is done the Utility A class shall be for dogs which have won the title C.D.X. and have not won the title U.D. Obedience judges and licensed handlers may not enter or handle dogs in this class. A dog may be handled in the Group Examination by a person other than the person who handled it in the individual exercises, but each dog must be handled in all exercises by the owner or by a member of his immediate family. All other dogs that are eligible for the Utility class but not eligible for the Utility A class may be entered only in the Utility B class to which the conditions listed in Section 24 shall apply. No dog may be entered in both Utility A and Utility B classes at any one trial.

SECTION 26 *Utility Exercises and Scores* The exercises and maximum scores in the Utility classes are:

1. Scent Discrimination— Article No. 1	30 points
2. Scent Discrimination— Article No. 2	30 points
3. Directed Retrieve	30 points
4. Signal Exercise	35 points
5. Directed Jumping	40 points
6. Group Examination	35 points
Maximum Total Score	200 points

SECTION 27   *U.D. Title*   The American Kennel Club will issue a Utility Dog certificate for each registered dog, and will permit the use of the letters 'U.D.' after the name of each dog that has been certified by three different judges of obedience trials to have received scores of more than 50 per cent of the available points in each of the six exercises and final scores of 170 or more points in Utility classes at three licensed or member obedience trials in each of which three or more dogs actually competed in the Utility class or classes.

SECTION 28   *Tracking Test*   This test shall be for dogs not less than six months of age, and must be judged by two judges. With each entry form for a licensed or member tracking test for a dog that has not passed a tracking test there must be filed a written statement, dated within six months of the date the entry is received, signed by a person who has been approved by The American Kennel Club to judge tracking tests, certifying that the dog is considered by him to be ready for such a test. These original statements cannot be used again and must be submitted to The American Kennel Club with the entry forms. Written permission to waive or modify this requirement may be granted by The American Kennel Club in unusual circumstances. Tracking tests are open to all dogs that are otherwise eligible under these Regulations.

This test cannot be given at a dog show or obedience trial. The duration of this test may be one day or more within a 15 day period after the original date in the event of an unusually large entry or other unforeseen emergency, provided that the change of date is satisfactory to the exhibitors affected.

SECTION 29   *T.D. Title*   The American Kennel Club will issue a Tracking Dog certificate to a registered dog, and will permit the use of the letters 'T.D.' after the name of each dog which has been certified by the two judges to have passed a licensed or member tracking test in which at least three dogs actually competed.

The owner of a dog holding both the U.D. and T.D. titles may use the letters 'U.D.T.' after the name of the Dog, signifying 'Utility Dog Tracker'.

SECTION 30   *Obedience Ribbons*   At licensed or member obedience trials the following colors shall be used for prize ribbons or rosettes in all regular classes:

First Prize	Blue
Second Prize	Red
Third Prize	Yellow
Fourth Prize	White
Special Prize	Dark Green

and the following colors shall be used for non-regular classes:

First Prize	Rose
Second Prize	Brown
Third Prize	Light Green
Fourth Prize	Gray

Each ribbon or rosette shall be at least two inches wide and approximately eight inches long, and shall bear on its face a facsimile of the seal of The American Kennel Club, the words 'Obedience Trial', the name of the prize, the name of the trial-giving club, the date of the trial, and the name of the city or town where the trial is given.

SECTION 31   *Match Ribbons*   If ribbons are given at sanctioned obedience matches they shall be of the following colors and shall have the words 'Obedience Match' printed on them, but may be of any design or size:

First Prize	Rose
Second Prize	Brown
Third Prize	Light Green
Fourth Prize	Gray
Special Prize	Green with pink edges

SECTION 32   *Prizes*   Ribbons for the four official placings and all other prizes offered for competition within a single regular class at a licensed or member trial, shall be awarded only to dogs that earn scores of more than 50 per cent of the available points in each exercise and final scores of 170 or more points.

Prizes for which dogs in one class compete against dogs in one or more other classes at a licensed or member trial may, at the option of the club holding the trial, specify that scores of more than 50 per cent of the available points in each exercise and final scores of 170 or more points, are required.

Ribbons and all prizes offered at sanctioned obedience matches, and in non-regular classes at licensed and member trials, shall be awarded on the basis of final scores without regard to more than 50 per cent of the points in each exercise.

Prizes at a licensed or member obedience trial must be offered to be won outright, with the exception that a prize which requires three wins by the same owner, not necessarily with the same dog, for permanent possession, may be offered for the dog with the highest qualifying score in one of the regular classes, for the highest scoring dog in the regular classes, or for the highest combined score in the Open B and Utility classes.

Subject to the provisions of paragraphs 1 and 2 of this section, prizes may be offered for the highest scoring dogs of the Groups as defined in Chapter 2 of the Dog Show Rules, or for the highest scoring dogs of any breed, but not for a breed variety. Show varieties are not recognised for obedience. In accordance with Chapter 2, all Poodles are in the Non-Sporting Group and all Manchester Terriers in the Terrier Group.

Prizes offered only to members of certain clubs or organizations will not be approved for publication in premium lists.

SECTION 33 *Risk* The owner or agent entering a dog in an obedience trial does so at his own risk and agrees to abide by the rules of The American Kennel Club, and the Obedience Regulations.

SECTION 34 *Decisions* At the trial the decisions of the judge shall be final in all matters affecting the scoring and the working of the dogs and their handlers. The Obedience Trial Committee, or the Bench Show Committee if the trial is held by a show-giving club, shall decide all other matters arising at the trial, including protests against dogs made under Chapter 20 of the Dog Show Rules, subject, however, to the rules and regulations of The American Kennel Club.

SECTION 35 *Dogs Must Compete* Any dog entered and received at a licensed or member obedience trial must compete in all exercises of all classes in which it is entered unless disqualified, expelled, or excused by the judge or by the Bench Show or Obedience Trial Committee, or unless excused by the official veterinarian to protect the health of the dog or of other dogs at the trial. The excuse of the official veterinarian must be in writing and must be approved

K

by the Superintendent or Show or Trial Secretary, and must be submitted to The American Kennel Club with the report of the trial. The judge must report to The American Kennel Club any dog that is not brought back for the group exercises.

SECTION 36 *Judging Program* Any club holding a licensed or member obedience trial must prepare, after the entries have closed, a program showing the time scheduled for the judging of each of the classes. A copy of this program shall be mailed to the owner of each entered dog and to each judge, and the program shall be printed in the catalog. This program shall be based on the judging of no more than 8 Novice entries, 7 Open entries, or 5 Utility entries, per hour during the time the show or trial will be open as published in the premium list, taking into consideration the starting hour for judging if published in the premium list, and the availability of rings. No judge shall be scheduled to exceed this rate of judging. In addition, one hour for rest or meals must be allowed if, under this formula, it will take more than five hours of actual judging to judge the dogs entered under him. No judge shall be assigned to judge for more than eight hours in one day under this formula, including any breed judging assignment if the obedience trial is held in conjunction with a dog show.

If any non-regular class is to be judged in the same ring as any regular class, or by the judge of any regular class, the non-regular class must be judged after the regular class.

SECTION 37 *Limitation of Entries* If a club holding a licensed or member trial anticipates an entry in excess of the club's facilities, it may limit entries in any or all classes by prominent announcement on the title or cover page of its premium list, or immediately under the obedience heading in the premium list for a dog show, stating that entries in one or more specified classes or in the obedience trial will automatically close when a certain limit or limits have been reached, even though the official closing date for entries has not arrived. If entries in the regular classes are limited, non-regular classes will not be approved.

SECTION 38 *Additional Judges, Reassignment, Split Classes* If when the entries have closed, it is found that the entry under one or more judges exceeds the limit established in Section 36, the club shall immediately secure the approval of The American Kennel Club for the appointment of one or more additional judges, or for reassignment of its advertised judges, so that no judge will be required to exceed the limit.

If a judge with an excessive entry was advertised to judge more than one class, one or more of his classes shall be assigned to another judge. The class or classes selected for reassignment shall first be any non-regular classes for which he was advertised, and shall then be those with the minimum number of entries which will bring the advertised judge's schedule within the maximum limit. If a judge with an excessive entry was advertised to judge only one class, the Superintendent, Show Secretary, or Obedience Trial Secretary, shall divide the entry as evenly as possible between the advertised judge and the other judge by drawing lots.

The club shall promptly mail to the owner of each affected entry, a notification of any change of judge. The owner shall be permitted to withdraw such entry at any time prior to the day of the show, and the entry fee shall then be refunded. If the entry in any one class is split in this manner, the advertised judge shall judge the run-off of any tie scores that may develop between the two groups of dogs, after each judge has first run-off any ties resulting from his own judging.

SECTION 39 *Split Classes in Premium List* A club may choose to announce two or more judges for any class in its premium list. In such case the entries shall be divided by lots as provided above, but no announcement of the drawing need be made to the owners in advance of the trial, and no owner shall be entitled to a refund of entry fee. In such case the premium list shall also specify the judge for the run-off of any tie scores which may develop between the dogs in the different groups, after each judge has first run-off any ties resulting from his own judging.

SECTION 40 *Split Classes, Official Ribbons* A club which gives a split class, whether the split is announced in the premium list or made after entries have closed, shall not award American Kennel Club official ribbons in either section, but may offer prizes on the basis of qualifying scores made within each section if the split class is announced in the premium list. The four dogs with the highest qualifying scores in the class regardless of the section in which they were made, shall be called back into the ring and awarded the four American Kennel Club official ribbons by one of the judges of the class who shall be responsible for recording the entry numbers of the four placed dogs in one of the judge's books.

SECTION 41 *Training of Dogs* There shall be no drilling nor intensive or corrective training of dogs on the grounds or premises at a licensed or member obedience trial. No practice rings or areas shall be permitted at such events. All dogs shall be kept on leash except when in the obedience ring or exercise ring. Spiked or other special training collars shall not be used on the grounds or premises at an obedience trial or match. These requirements shall not be interpreted as preventing a handler from moving normally about the grounds or premises with his dog at heel on leash, nor from giving such signals or such commands in a normal tone, as are necessary and usual in everyday life in heeling a dog or making it stay, but physical or verbal disciplining of dogs shall not be permitted except to a reasonable extent in the case of an attack on a person or another dog. The Superintendent, or Show or Trial Secretary, and the members of the Bench Show or Obedience Trial Committee, shall be responsible for compliance with this section, and shall investigate any reports of infractions.

SECTION 42 *Abuse of Dogs* The Bench Show or Obedience Trial Committee shall also investigate any reports of abuse of dogs or severe disciplining of dogs on the grounds or premises of a show, trial, or match. Any person who, at a licensed or member obedience trial, conducts himself in such manner or in any other manner prejudicial to the best interests of the sport, or who fails to comply with the requirements of Section 41 above after receiving a warning, shall be dealt with promptly, during the trial if possible, after the offender has been notified of the specific charges against him, and has been given an opportunity to be heard in his own defense, in accordance with Section 43 below.

Article XII Section 2 of the Constitution and By-Laws of The American Kennel Club provides:

SECTION 43 *Discipline* The Bench Show, Obedience Trial or Field Trial Committee of a club or association shall have the right to suspend any person from the privileges of The American Kennel Club for conduct prejudicial to the best interests of pure-bred dogs, dog shows, obedience trials, field trials or The American Kennel Club, alleged to have occurred in connection with or during the progress of its show, obedience trial or field trial, after the alleged offender has been given an opportunity to be heard.

Notice in writing must be sent promptly by registered mail by the Bench Show, Obedience Trial or Field Trial Committee to the person suspended and a duplicate notice giving the name and address of the person suspended and full details as to the reasons for the suspension must be forwarded to The American Kennel Club within seven days.

An appeal may be taken from a decision of a Bench Show, Obedience Trial or Field Trial Committee. Notice in writing claiming such appeal together with a deposit of five ($5.00) dollars must be sent to The American Kennel Club within thirty days after the date of suspension. The Board of Directors may itself hear said appeal or may refer it to a committee of the Board, or to a Trial Board to be heard. The deposit shall become the property of The American Kennel Club if the decision is confirmed, or shall be returned to the appellant if the decision is not confirmed.

(*See Guide for Bench Show and Obedience Trial Committees in Dealing with Misconduct at Dog Shows and Obedience Trials for procedure to be followed at licensed or member obedience trials.*)

(*The Committee at a Sanctioned event does not have this power of suspension, but must investigate any allegation of such conduct and forward a complete and detailed report of any such incident to The American Kennel Club.*)

CHAPTER 2

Regulations for Performance

SECTION 1   *Ring Conditions*   If the judging takes place indoors the ring should be rectangular and should be at least 35 feet wide and 50 feet long for all obedience classes. In no case shall the ring for a Utility class be less than 35 feet by 50 feet, and in no case shall the ring for a Novice or Open class be less than 30 feet by 40 feet. The floor shall have a surface or covering that provides firm footing for the largest dogs, and rubber or similar non-slip material must be laid for the take off and landing at all jumps unless the surface, in the judge's opinion, is such as not to require it. At an outdoor show or trial the rings shall be about 40 feet wide and 50 feet long. The ground shall be clean and level, and the grass, if any, shall be cut short. The Club and Superintendent are responsible for providing, for the Open classes, an appropriate place approved by the judge, for the handlers to go completely out of sight of their dogs. If inclement weather at an outdoor trial necessitates the judging of obedience under shelter, the requirements as to ring size may be waived.

SECTION 2 *Obedience Rings at Dog Shows* At an outdoor dog show a separate ring or rings shall be provided for obedience, and a sign forbidding anyone to permit any dog to use the ring, except when being judged, shall be set up in each such ring by the Superintendent or Show Secretary. It shall be his duty as well as that of the Show Committee to enforce this regulation. At an indoor show where limited space does not permit the exclusive use of any ring for obedience, the same regulation will apply after the obedience rings have been set up. At a dog show the material used for enclosing the obedience rings shall be at least equal to the material used for enclosing the breed rings. The ring must be thoroughly cleaned before the obedience judging starts if it has previously been used for breed judging.

SECTION 3 *Compliance with Regulations and Standards* In accordance with the certification on the entry form, the handler of each dog and the person signing each entry form must be familiar with the Obedience Regulations applicable to the class in which the dog is entered. A handler who cannot actually walk about the ring as required by these regulations, without assistance or without special directions from another person, is ineligible to handle a dog in the obedience ring at a licensed or member trial.

SECTION 4 *Praise and Handling between Exercises* Praise and patting are allowed between exercises, but points must be deducted from the total score for a dog that is not under reasonable control while being praised. A handler must not carry or offer food in the ring.

Imperfections in heeling between exercises will not be judged. In the Novice classes the dog may be guided gently by the collar between exercises and to get it into proper position for the next exercise. There shall be a substantial penalty for any dog that is picked up or carried at any time in the obedience ring, and for a dog in the Open or Utility classes that is not readily controllable or that is physically controlled at any time, except for permitted patting between exercises. Minor penalties shall be imposed for a dog that does not respond promptly to its handler's commands or signals between exercises in the Open and Utility classes.

SECTION 5   *Use of Leash*   All dogs shall be kept on leash except when in the obedience ring or exercise ring. Dogs should be brought into the ring and taken out of the ring on leash. Dogs may be kept on leash in the ring when brought in to receive awards, and when waiting in the ring before and after the group exercises. The leash shall be left on the judge's table between the individual exercises, and during all exercises except the Heel on Leash and group exercises. The leash may be of fabric or leather and, in the Novice classes, shall be of sufficient length to provide adequate slack in the Heel on Leash exercise.

SECTION 6   *Collars*   Dogs in the obedience ring must wear well-fitting plain buckle or slip collars of leather, fabric, or chain. Fancy collars, spiked collars or other special training collars, or collars that are either too tight or so large that they hang down unreasonably in front of the dogs are not permitted, nor may there be anything hanging from the collars.

SECTION 7   *Misbehavior*   Any disciplining by the handler in the ring, any display of fear or nervousness by the dog, or any uncontrolled behavior of the dog such as snapping, barking, relieving itself in the ring, or running away from its handler, whether it occurs during an exercise, between exercises, or before or after judging, must be penalized according to the seriousness of the misbehavior, and the judge may expel or excuse the dog from further competition in the class. If such behavior occurs during an exercise, the penalty must first be applied to the score for that exercise. Should the penalty be greater than the value of the exercise during which it is incurred, the additional points shall be deducted from the total score under Misbehavior. If such behavior occurs before or after the judging or between exercises, the entire penalty shall be deducted from the total score.

SECTION 8 *Commands and Signals* Whenever a command or signal is mentioned in these regulations, a single command or signal only may be given by the handler, and any extra commands or signals must be penalized; except that whenever the regulations specify 'command and/or signal' the handler may give either one or the other or both command and signal simultaneously. When a signal is permitted and given, it must be a single gesture with one arm and hand only, and the arm must immediately be returned to its normal position. Delay in following a judge's order to give a command or signal must be penalized, unless the delay is directed by the judge because of some distraction or interference.

The signal for downing a dog may be given either with the arm raised or with a down swing of the arm, but any pause in holding the arm upright followed by a down swing of the arm will be considered an additional signal.

Signaling correction to a dog is forbidden and must be penalized. Signals must be inaudible and the handler must not touch the dog. Any unusual noise or motion may be considered to be a signal. Movements of the body shall be considered additional signals except that a handler may bend as far as necessary to bring his hand on a level with the dog's eyes in giving a signal to a dog in the heel position, and that in the Directed Retrieve exercise the body and knees may be bent to the extent necessary to give the direction to the dog. Whistling or the use of a whistle is prohibited.

The dog's name may be used once immediately before any verbal command or before a verbal command and signal when these regulations permit command and/or signal. The name shall not be used with any signal not given simultaneously with a verbal command. The dog's name, when given immediately before a verbal command, shall not be considered as an additional command, but a dog that responds to its name without waiting for the verbal command shall be scored as having anticipated the command. The dog should never anticipate the handler's directions, but must wait for the appropriate commands and/or signals.

Loud commands by handlers to their dogs create a poor impression of obedience and should be avoided. Shouting is not necessary even in a noisy place if the dog is properly trained to respond to a normal tone of voice. Commands which in the judge's opinion are excessively loud will be penalized.

SECTION 9 *Heel Position* The heel position as used in these regulations, whether the dog is sitting, standing, or moving at heel, means that the dog shall be straight in line with the direction in which the handler is facing, at the handler's left side, and as close as practicable to the handler's left leg without crowding, permitting the handler freedom of motion at all times. The area from the dog's head to shoulder shall be in line with the handler's left hip.

SECTION 10 *Heel on Leash* The handler shall enter the ring with his dog on a loose leash and shall stand still with the dog sitting in the heel position until the judge asks if the handler is ready and then gives the order 'Forward'. The handler may give the command or signal to Heel, and shall start walking briskly and in a natural manner with the dog on loose leash. The dog shall walk close to the left side of the handler without crowding, permitting the handler freedom of motion at all times. At each order to 'Halt', the handler will stop and his dog shall sit straight and smartly in the Heel position without command or signal and shall not move until ordered to do so. It is permissible after each Halt before moving again, for the handler to give the command or signal to Heel.

The leash may be held in either hand or in both hands, at the handler's option, provided the hands are in a natural position. However, the handler and dog will be penalized if, in the judge's opinion, the leash is used to signal or give assistance to the dog.

Any tightening or jerking of the leash or any act, signal or command which in the opinion of the judge gives the dog assistance shall be penalized. The judge will give the orders 'Forward', 'Halt', 'Right turn', 'Left turn', 'About turn', 'Slow', 'Normal', and 'Fast', which order signifies that both the handler and dog must run, changing pace and moving forward at noticeably accelerated speed. These orders may be given in any sequence and may be repeated if necesary. In executing the About Turn, the handler will do a Right About Turn in all cases. The judge will say 'Exercise finished' after the heeling and then 'Are you ready?' before starting the Figure Eight.

The judge will order the handler to execute the 'Figure Eight' which signifies that the handler shall walk around and between the two stewards who shall stand about 8 feet apart, or if there is only one steward, shall walk around and between the judge and the steward. The Figure Eight in the Novice classes shall be done on leash only. The handler may choose to go in either direction. There shall be no About Turn in the Figure Eight, but the handler and dog shall go twice completely around the Figure Eight with at least one Halt during and another Halt at the end of the exercise.

SECTION 11   *Stand for Examination*   The judge will give the order for examination and the handler will stand or pose his dog off leash, give the command and/or signal to Stay, walk forward at least six feet in front of his dog, turn around, and stand facing his dog. The method by which the dog is made to stand or pose is optional with the handler who may take any reasonable time in posing the dog, as in the show ring, before deciding to give the command and/or signal to stay. The judge will approach the dog from the front and will touch its head, body and hindquarters only, and will then give the order 'Back to your dog', whereupon the handler will walk around behind his dog to the heel position. The dog must remain in a standing position until the judge says 'Exercise finished'. The dog must show no shyness nor resentment at any time during the exercise.

SECTION 12   *Heel Free*   This shall be executed in the same manner as Heel on Leash except that the dog is off the leash. Heeling in both Novice and Open classes is done in the same manner except that in the Open classes all work is done off leash, including the Figure Eight.

SECTION 13   *Recall and Drop on Recall*   To execute the Recall to handler, upon order or signal from the judge 'Leave your dog', the dog is given the command and/or signal to stay in the sitting position while the handler walks towards the other end of the ring, the distance to be about 40 feet. Upon order or signal from the judge 'Call your dog', the handler calls or signals the dog, which in the Novice class must come straight in at a brisk pace and sit straight, centred immediately in front of the handler's feet and close enough so that the handler could readily touch its head without moving either foot or having to stretch forward. The dog shall not touch the handler nor sit between his feet. Upon order or signal from the judge to 'Finish', the dog on command or signal must go smartly to the heel position and sit.

In the Open class, at a point designated by the judge, the dog must drop completely to a down position immediately on command or signal from the handler, and must remain in the down position until, on order or signal from the judge, the handler calls or signals the dog which must rise and complete the exercise as in the Novice class. The method by which the dog goes to the heel position shall be optional with the handler provided it is done smartly and the dog sits straight at heel.

SECTION 14 *Long Sit* In the Long Sit in the Novice classes all the competing dogs in the class take the exercise together, except that if there are 12 or more dogs they shall, at the judge's option, be judged in groups of not less than 6 nor more than 15 dogs. Where the same judge does both classes the separate classes may be combined provided there are not more than 15 dogs competing in the two classes combined. The dogs that are in the ring shall be lined up in catalog order along one of the four sides of the ring. Handler's armbands, weighted with leashes or other articles if necessary, shall be placed behind the dogs. On order from the judge the handlers shall sit their dogs, if they are not already sitting, and on further order from the judge to 'Leave your dogs' the handlers shall give the command and/or signal to Stay and immediately leave their dogs, go to the opposite side of the ring, and line up facing their respective dogs. After one minute from the time he has ordered the handlers to leave their dogs, the judge will order the handlers 'Back to your dogs' whereupon the handlers must return promptly to their dogs, each walking around and in back of his own dog to the heel position. The dogs must not move from the sitting position until after the judge says 'Exercise finished'.

SECTION 15 *Long Down* The Long Down in the Novice classes is done in the same manner as the Long Sit except that instead of sitting the dogs the handlers, on order from the judge, will down their dogs without touching the dogs or their collars, and except further that the judge will order the handlers back after three minutes. The dogs must stay in the down position until after the judge says 'Exercise finished'.

SECTION 16 *Open Classes, Long Sit and Long Down* These exercises in the Open classes are performed in the same manner as in the Novice classes except that after leaving their dogs the handlers must cross to the opposite side of the ring, and then leave the ring in single file as directed by the judge and go to a place designated by the judge, completely out of sight of their dogs, where they must remain until called by the judge after the expiration of the time limit of three minutes in the Long Sit and five minutes in the Long Down, from the time the judge gave the order to 'Leave your dogs'. On order from the judge the handlers shall return to the ring in single file in reverse order, lining up facing their dogs at the opposite side of the ring, and returning to their dogs on order from the judge.

SECTION 17 *Retrieve on the Flat* In retrieving the dumbbell on the flat, the handler stands with his dog sitting at the heel position in a place designated by the judge, and the judge gives the orders 'Throw it', whereupon the handler may give the command and/or signal to Stay, which may not be given with the hand that is holding the dumbbell, and throws the dumbbell; 'Send your dog', whereupon the handler gives the command or signal to his dog to retrieve; 'Take it', whereupon the handler may give a command or signal and takes the dumbbell from the dog; 'Finish', whereupon the handler gives the command or signal to heel as in the Recall. The dog shall not move forward to retrieve nor deliver to hand on return until given the command or signal by the handler following order by the judge. The retrieve shall be executed at a fast trot or gallop, without unnecessary mouthing or playing with the dumbbell. The dog shall sit straight, centered immediately in front of its handler's feet and close enough so that the handler can readily take the dumbbell without moving either foot or having to stretch forward. The dog shall not touch the handler nor sit between his feet.

The dumbbell, which must be approved by the judge, shall be made of one or more pieces of one of the heavy hardwoods, which shall not be hollowed out. It may be unfinished, or coated with a clear finish, or painted white. It shall have no decorations or attachments but may bear an inconspicuous mark for identification. The size of the dumbbell shall be proportionate to the size of the dog. The judge shall require the dumbbell to be thrown again before the dog is sent if, in his opinion, it is thrown too short a distance, or too far to one side, or against the ringside.

SECTION 18 *Retrieve over High Jump* In retrieving the dumbbell over the High Jump, the exercise is executed in the same manner as the Retrieve on the Flat, except that the dog must jump the High Jump both going and coming. The High Jump shall be jumped clear and the jump shall be as nearly as possible one and one-half times the height of the dog at the withers, as determined by the judge, with a minimum height of 8 inches and a maximum height of 36 inches. This applies to all breeds except those listed below for which the jump shall be once the height of the dog at the withers or three feet, whichever is less: Bloodhounds, Bullmastiffs, Great Danes, Great Pyrenees, Mastiffs, Newfoundlands and St. Bernards.

The handler has the option of standing any reasonable distance from the High Jump, but must stay in the same spot throughout the exercise.

The side posts of the High Jump shall be 4 feet high and the jump shall be 5 feet wide and shall be so constructed as to provide adjustment for each 2 inches from 8 inches to 36 inches. It is suggested that the jump have a bottom board 8 inches wide including the space from the bottom of the board to the ground or floor, together with three other 8 inch boards, one 4 inch board, and one 2 inch board. The jump shall be painted a flat white. The width in inches, and nothing else, shall be painted on each side of each board in black 2 inch figures, the figure on the bottom board representing the distance from the ground or floor to the top of the board.

SECTION 19 *Broad Jump* In the Broad Jump the handler will stand with his dog sitting at the heel position in front of and anywhere within 10 feet of the jump. On order from the judge to 'Leave your dog', the handler will give his dog the command and/or signal to stay, and go to a position facing the right side of the jump, with his toes about 2 feet from the jump, and within the range of the first and last hurdles. On order from the judge the handler shall give the command or signal to jump and the dog shall clear the entire distance of the Broad Jump without touching and, without further command or signal, return to a sitting position immediately in front of the handler as in the Recall. The handler shall change his position by executing a right angle turn while the dog is in mid-air, but shall remain in the same spot. On order from the judge, the handler will give the command or signal to Heel and the dog shall finish as in the Recall.

The Broad Jump shall consist of four hurdles, built to telescope for convenience, made of boards about 8 inches wide, the largest measuring about 5 feet in length and 6 inches high at the highest point, all painted a flat white. When set up they shall be arranged in order of size and shall be evenly spaced so as to cover a distance equal to twice the height of the High Jump as set for the particular dog, with the low side of each hurdle and the lowest hurdle nearest the dog. The four hurdles shall be used for a jump of 52 inches to 72 inches, three for a jump of 32 inches to 48 inches, and two for a jump of 16 inches to 28 inches. The highest hurdles shall be removed first.

SECTION 20 *Scent Discrimination* In each of these two exercises the dog must select by scent alone and retrieve an article which has been handled by its handler. The articles shall be provided by the handler and these shall consist of two sets, each comprised of five identical articles not more than six inches in length, which may be items of everyday use. One set shall be made entirely of rigid metal, and one of leather of such design that nothing but leather is visible except for the minimum amount of thread or metal necessary to hold the article together. The articles in each set must be legibly numbered each with a different number, and must be approved by the judge.

The handler shall present all 10 articles to the judge and the judge shall designate one article from each of the two sets, and shall make a written note of the numbers of the two articles he selects. These two handler's articles shall be placed on a table or chair in the ring until picked up by the handler who shall hold in his hand only one article at a time. The handler's scent may be imparted to the article only from his hands which must remain in plain sight. The handler has the option as to which article he picks up first. Before the start of the Scent Discrimination exercises the judge or the steward will handle each of the remaining 8 articles before placing them at random in the ring about 6 inches apart. The handler will stand about 15 feet from the articles with the dog sitting at heel position with their backs to the articles. On order from the judge, the handler immediately will place his article on the judge's book or work sheet and the judge, without touching the article with his hands, will place it among the other articles.

On order from the judge to 'Send your dog', the handler and dog will execute a Right About Turn to face the articles and the handler will simultaneously give the command or signal to retrieve. The dog shall not again sit after turning, but shall go directly to the articles. The handler may give his scent to the dog by gently touching the dog's nose with the palm of one open hand, but this may only be done while the dog is sitting at heel and the hand must be returned to the handler's side before handler and dog turn to face the articles. The dog shall go at a brisk pace to the articles. It may take any reasonable time to select the right article, but only provided it works continuously and does not pick up any other article other than the one with its handler's scent. After picking up the right article the dog shall return at a brisk pace and complete the exercise as in the Retrieve on the Flat.

The same procedure is followed in each of the two Scent Discrimination exercises. Should a dog retrieve a wrong article in the first exercise, it shall be placed on the table or chair, and the handler's article must also be taken up from the remaining articles. The second exercise shall then be completed with one less article in the ring.

SECTION 21 *Directed Retrieve* In this exercise the handler will stand with his dog sitting in the heel position, midway between the two jumps. The handler will provide three short, predominantly white, work gloves, which must be open and must be approved by the judge. The judge or steward shall place the three gloves across the end of the ring in front of the handler and dog, one in each corner and one in the center, about three feet from the end and/or side of the ring. There shall be no table or chair at this end of the ring.

The judge will give the order 'Left' or 'Right' or 'Center'. The handler must give the command to Heel and turn with his dog to face the designated glove, if necessary, but may not turn completely around nor touch the dog to get it in position. The handler will then give his dog the direction to the designated glove with his left hand and arm, and the command to retrieve. The dog shall go directly to the glove at a brisk pace and retrieve it without unnecessary mouthing or playing with it, completing the exercise as in Retrieve on the Flat.

The handler may bend his knees and body in giving the direction to the dog and in giving the command to retrieve, after which the handler will stand erect with his arms at his sides. The exercise shall consist of a single retrieve, but the judge shall designate different glove positions for successive dogs.

SECTION 22 *Signal Exercise* In the Signal Exercise the heeling is done in the same manner as in the Heel Free exercise except that throughout the entire exercise the handler uses signals only and must not speak to his dog at any time. On order from the judge 'Forward', the handler signals his dog to walk at heel and then, on specific order from the judge in each case, the handler and the dog execute a 'Left turn', 'Right turn', About turn', 'Halt', 'Slow', 'Normal', 'Fast'. These orders may be given in any sequence and may be repeated if necessary. Then on order from the judge, and while the dog is walking at heel, the handler signals his dog to Stand in the heel position near the end of the ring, and on further order from the judge 'Leave your dog', the handler signals his dog to Stay, goes to the far end of the ring, and turns to face his dog. Then on separate and specific signals from the judge in each case, the handler will give the signals to Drop, to Sit, to Come and to Finish as in the Recall. During the heeling part of this exercise the handler may not give any signal except where a command or signal is permitted in the Heeling exercises.

SECTION 23 *Directed Jumping* In the Directed Jumping exercise the jumps shall be placed midway in the ring at right angles to the sides of the ring and 18 to 20 feet apart, the Bar Jump on one side, the High Jump on the other. The handler from a position on the center line of the ring and about 20 feet from the line of the jumps, stands with his dog sitting in the heel position. On order from the judge 'Send your dog', he commands and/or signals his dog to go forward at a brisk pace towards the other end of the ring to an equal distance beyond the jumps and in the approximate center where the handler gives the command to Sit, whereupon the dog must stop and sit with its attention on the handler, but need not sit squarely. The judge will then designate which jump is to be taken first by the dog, whereupon the handler commands and/or signals his dog to return to him over the designated jump, the dog sitting in front of the handler and finishing as in the Recall. While the dog is in mid-air the handler may turn so as to be facing the dog as it returns. The judge will say 'Exercise finished' after the dog has returned to the heel position. When the dog is again sitting in the heel position for the second part of the exercise, the judge will ask 'Are you ready?' before giving the order 'Send your dog' for the second jump. The same procedure is to be followed for the dog taking the opposite jump. It is optional with the judge which jump is taken first but both jumps must be taken to complete the exercise and the judge must not designate the jump until the dog is at the far end of the ring.

The height of the jumps shall be the same as required in the Open classes. The High Jump shall be the same as that used in the Open classes, and the Bar Jump shall consist of a bar between 2 and 2½ inches square with the four edges rounded sufficiently to remove any sharpness. The bar shall be painted a flat black and white in alternate sections of about 3 inches each. The bar shall be supported by two unconnected 4 foot upright posts about 5 feet apart. The bar shall be adjustable for each 2 inches of height from 8 inches to 36 inches, and the jump shall be so constructed and positioned that the bar can be knocked off without disturbing the uprights. The dog shall clear the jumps without touching them.

SECTION 24 *Group Examination* All the competing dogs take this exercise together, except that if there are 12 or more dogs, they shall be judged in groups of not less than 6 nor more than 15 dogs, at the judge's option. The handlers and dogs that are in the ring shall line up in catalog order, side by side down the center of the ring with the dogs at heel position. Each handler shall place his armband, weighted with leash or other article, if necessary, behind his dog. On order from the judge to 'Stand your dogs', all the handlers will stand or pose their dogs, and on order from the judge 'Leave your dogs', all the handlers will give the command and/or signal to Stay, walk forward to the side of the ring, then about turn and face their dogs. The judge will approach each dog in turn from the front and examine it, going over the dog with his

L

hands as in dog show judging. When all dogs have been examined, and after the handlers have been away from their dogs for at least three minutes, the judge will promptly order the handlers 'Back to your dogs', and the handlers will walk around behind their dogs to the heel position, after which the judge will say 'Exercise finished'. Each dog must remain standing at its position in the line from the time its handler leaves it until the end of the exercise, and must show no shyness nor resentment.

SECTION 25 *Tracking* The tracking test must be performed with the dog on leash, the length of the track to be not less than 440 yards nor more than 500 yards, the scent to be not less than one half hour nor more than two hours old and that of a stranger who will leave an inconspicuous glove or wallet, dark in color, at the end of the track where it must be found by the dog and picked up by the dog or handler. The article must be approved in advance by the judges. The tracklayer will follow the track which has been staked out with flags a day or more earlier, collecting all the flags on the way with the exception of one flag at the start of the track and one flag about 30 yards from the start of the track to indicate the direction of the track; then deposit the article at the end of the track and leave the course, proceeding straight ahead at least 50 feet. The tracklayer must wear his own shoes which, if not having leather soles, must have uppers of fabric or leather. The dog shall wear a harness to which is attached a leash between 20 and 40 feet in length. The handler shall follow the dog at a distance of not less than 20 feet, and the dog shall not be guided by the handler. The dog may be restrained by the handler, but any leading or guiding of the dog constitutes grounds for calling the handler off and marking the dog 'Failed'. A dog may, at the handler's option, be given one, and only one, second chance to take the scent between the two flags, provided it has not passed the second flag.

The Club or Tracking Test Secretary, after a licensed or member tracking test, shall forward the two copies of the judges' marked charts, the entry forms with certifications attached, and a marked and certified copy of the catalog pages or sheets listing the dogs entered in the tracking test, to The American Kennel Club so as to reach its office within seven days after the close of the test.

CHAPTER 3

Regulations for Judging

SECTION 1 *Standardized Judging* Standardized judging is of paramount importance. Judges are not permitted to inject their own variations into the exercises, but must see that each handler and dog executes the various exercises exactly as described in these regulations. A handler who is familiar with these regulations should be able to enter the ring under any judge without having to inquire how the particular judge wishes to have any exercise performed, and without being confronted with some unexpected requirement.

SECTION 2 *Judge's Report on Ring and Equipment* The Superintendent and the officials of the club holding the obedience trial are responsible for providing rings and equipment which meet the requirements of these regulations. However, the judge must check the ring and equipment provided for his use before starting to judge, and must report to The American Kennel Club after the trial any undesirable ring conditions or deficiencies that have not been promptly corrected at his request.

SECTION 3 *Stewards* The judge is in sole charge of his ring until his assignment is completed. Stewards are provided to assist him, but they may act only on the judge's instructions. Stewards shall not give information or instructions to owners and handlers except as specifically instructed by the judge, and then only in such a manner that it is clear that the instructions are those of the judge.

SECTION 4 *Training and Disciplining in the Ring* The judge shall not permit any handler to train his dog nor to practice any exercise in the ring either before or after he is judged, and shall deduct points from the total score of any dog whose handler does this. A handler who disciplines his dog in the ring must be severely penalized. The penalty shall be deducted from the points available for the exercise during which the disciplining may occur, and additional points may be deducted from the total score if necessary. If the disciplining does not occur during an exercise the penalty shall be deducted from the total score. Any abuse of a dog in the ring must be immediately reported by the judge to the Bench Show or Obedience Trial Committee for action under Chapter 1, Section 43.

SECTION 5 *Catalog Order* Dogs should be judged in catalog order to the extent that it is practicable to do so without holding up the judging in any ring for a dog that is entered in more than one class at the show or trial.

Judges are not required to wait for dogs for either the individual exercises or the group exercises. It is the responsibility of each contestant to be ready with his dog at ringside when required, without waiting to be called. The judge's first consideration should be the convenience of those exhibitors who are at ringside with their dogs when scheduled, and who ask no favors.

A judge may agree, on request in advance, to judge a dog earlier or later than the time scheduled by catalog order if the same dog is entered in another class which may conflict. However, a judge should not hesitate to mark absent and to refuse to judge any dog and handler that are not at ringside ready to be judged in catalog order if no such arrangement has been made in advance, nor if the dog is available while its handler is occupied with some other dog or dogs at the show or trial.

SECTION 6 *Judge's Book and Score Sheets* The judge must enter the scores and sub-total score of each dog in the official judge's book immediately after each dog has been judged on the individual exercises and before judging the next dog. Scores for the group exercises and total scores must be entered in the official judge's book immediately after each group of dogs has been judged. No score may be changed except to correct an arithmetical error or if a score has been entered in the wrong column. All final scores must be entered in the judge's book before prizes are awarded. No person other than the judge may make any entry in the judge's book. Judges may use separate score sheets for their own purposes, but shall not give out nor allow exhibitors to see such sheets, nor give out any other written scores, nor permit anyone else to distribute score sheets or cards prepared by the judge. Carbon copies of the sheets in the official judge's book shall be made available through the Superintendent or Show or Trial Secretary for examination by owners and handlers immediately after the prizes have been awarded in each class. If score cards are distributed by a club after the prizes are awarded they must contain no more information than is shown in the judge's book and must be marked 'unofficial score'.

SECTION 7 *Announcement of Scores* The judge shall not disclose any score or partial score to contestants or spectators until he has completed the judging of the entire class or, in case of a split class, until he has completed the judging of his division; nor shall he permit anyone else to do so. After all the scores are recorded for the class, or for the division in case of a split class, the judge shall call for all available dogs that have won qualifying scores to be brought into the ring. Before awarding the prizes, the judge shall inform the spectators as to the maximum number of points for a perfect score, and shall then announce the score of each prize winner, and announce to the handler the score of each dog that has won a qualifying score.

SECTION 8 *Explanations and Errors* The judge is not required to explain his scoring, and should not enter into any discussion with any contestant who appears to be dissatisfied. Any interested person who thinks that there may have been an arithmetical error or an error in identifying a dog may report the facts to one of the stewards or to the Superintendent or Show or Trial Secretary so that the matter may be checked.

SECTION 9 *Rejudging* If a dog has failed in a particular part of an exercise, it shall not ordinarily be rejudged nor given a second chance; but if in the judge's opinion the dog's performance was prejudiced by peculiar and unusual conditions, the judge may at his own discretion rejudge the dog on the entire exercise.

SECTION 10 *Ties* In case of a tie for any prize in a class, the dogs shall be tested again by having them perform at the same time all or some part of one or more of the regular exercises in that class. In the Utility class the dogs shall perform at the same time all or some part of the Signal exercise. The original scores shall not be changed.

SECTION 11 *Judge's Directions* The judge's orders and signals should be given to the handlers in a clear and understandable manner, but in such a way that the work of the dog is not disturbed. Before starting each exercise, the judge shall ask 'Are you ready?. At the end of each exercise the judge shall say 'Exercise finished'. Each contestant must be worked and judged separately except for the Long Sit, Long Down, and Group Examination exercises, and in running off a tie.

SECTION 12 *A and B Classes and Different Breeds* The same methods and standards must be used for judging and scoring the A and B Classes, and in judging and scoring the work of dogs of different breeds.

SECTION 13 *No Added Requirements* No judge shall require any dog or handler to do anything, nor penalize a dog or handler for failing to do anything, that is not required by these regulations.

SECTION 14 *Additional Commands or Signals and Interference* If a handler gives an additional command or signal not permitted by these regulations, either when no command or signal is permitted, or simultaneously with or following a permitted command or signal, or if he uses the dog's name with a permitted signal but without a permitted command, the dog shall be scored as though it had failed completely to perform that particular part of the exercise. A judge who is aware of any assistance, interference, or attempts to control a dog from outside the ring, must act promptly to stop any such double handling or interference, and should penalize the dog or give it less than a qualifying score if in his opinion it received such aid.

SECTION 15 *Standard of Perfection* The judge must carry a mental picture of the theoretically perfect performance in each exercise and score each dog and handler against this visualized standard which shall combine the utmost in willingness, enjoyment and precision on the part of the dog, and naturalness, gentleness, and smoothness in handling. Lack of willingness or enjoyment on the part of the dog must be penalized, as must lack of precision in the dog's performance, and roughness in handling. There shall be no penalty of less than $\frac{1}{2}$ point or multiple of $\frac{1}{2}$ point.

SECTION 16 *Qualifying Performance* A judge's certification in his judge's book of a qualifying score for any particular dog constitutes his certification to The American Kennel Club that the dog on this particular occasion has performed all of the required exercises at least in accordance with the minimum standards and that its performance on this occasion would justify the awarding of the obedience title associated with the particular class. A qualifying score must never be awarded to a dog whose performance has not met the minimum requirements, nor to a dog that shows fear or resentment, or that relieves itself at any time in an indoor ring, or that relieves itself while performing any exercise indoors or outdoors, nor to a dog whose handler disciplines or abuses it in the ring, or carries or offers food in the ring.

In deciding whether the faulty performance of a particular exercise by a particular dog warrants a qualifying score or a score that is something less than 50 per cent of the available points, the judge shall consider whether the awarding of an obedience title would be justified if all dogs competing in the class performed the exercise in a similar manner; and must give a score of less than 50 per cent of the available points if he decides that it would be contrary to the best interests of the sport if all dogs competing in the class performed in a similar manner on all occasions.

SECTION 17 *Orders and Minimum Penalties* The orders for the exercises and the standards for judging are set forth in the following sections. The list of faults are not intended to be complete but minimum penalties are specified for most of the more common and serious faults. There is no maximum limit on penalties. A dog which makes none of the errors listed may still fail to qualify or may be scored zero for other reasons.

SECTION 18 *Heel on Leash* The orders for this exercise are 'Forward', 'Halt', 'Right turn', 'Left turn', 'About turn', 'Slow', 'Normal', 'Fast', 'Figure eight'. These orders may be given in any order and may be repeated, if necessary, but the judge shall attempt to standardize the heeling pattern for all dogs in any class. The principal feature of this exercise is the ability of the dog to work as a team with its handler. A dog that is unmanageable must be scored zero. Where a handler continually tugs on the leash or adapts his pace to that of the dog, the judge must score such a dog less than 50 per cent of the available points. Substantial deductions shall be made for additional commands or signals to Heel and for failure of dog or handler to change pace noticeably for Slow and Fast. Minor deductions shall be made for such things as poor sits, occasionally guiding the dog with the leash, heeling wide, and other imperfections in heeling. In judging this exercise the judge shall follow the handler at a discreet distance so that he may observe any signals or commands given by the handler to the dog, but without interfering with either dog or handler.

SECTION 19 *Stand for Examination* The orders for this exercise are 'Stand your dog for examination', 'Back to your dog'. The principal features of this exercise are to stand in position before and during examination and to show no shyness nor resentment. A dog that sits before or during the examination or growls or snaps must be marked zero. A dog that moves away from the place where it was left before or during the examination, or a dog that shows any shyness or resentment, must receive less than 50 per cent of the available points. Depending on the circumstances in each case, minor or susbtantial deductions must be made for any dog that moves its feet at any time, or that sits, or moves away after the examination is completed. The examination shall consist of touching only the dog's head, body and hindquarters with the fingers and palm of one hand. The scoring of this exercise will not start until the handler has given the command and/or signal to Stay, except for such things as rough treatment of the dog by its handler or active resistance by the dog to its handler's attempts to make it stand, which shall be penalized substantially.

SECTION 20 *Heel Free* The orders and scoring for this exercise shall be the same as for Heel on Leash except that the Figure Eight is omitted in the Heel Free exercise in the Novice classes.

SECTION 21 *Recall* The orders for this exercise are 'Leave your dog', 'Call your dog', 'Finish'. The principal features of this exercise are the prompt response to the handler's command or signal to Come, and the Stay from the time the handler leaves the dog until he calls it. A dog that does not come on the first command or signal must be scored zero. A dog that does not stay without extra command or signal, or that moves from the place where it was left, from the time the handler leaves until it is called, or that does not come close enough so that the handler could readily touch its head without moving either foot or having to stretch forward, must receive less than 50 per cent of the points. Substantial deductions shall be made for a slow response to the Come, depending on the specific circumstances in each case; for extra commands or signals to Stay if given before the handler leaves the dog; for a dog that stands or lies down; for extra commands or signals to Finish; and for failure to Sit or Finish. Minor deductions shall be made for poor or slow Sits or Finishes and for a dog that touches the handler on coming in or sits between his feet.

SECTION 22 *Long Sit and Long Down* The orders for these exercises are 'Sit your dogs' or 'Down your dogs', 'Leave your dogs', 'Back to your dogs'. The principal features of these exercises are to stay, and to remain in the sitting or down position, whichever is required by the particular exercise. A dog that at any time during the exercise moves a substantial distance away from the place where it was left, or that goes over to any other dog, must be marked zero. A dog that stays on the spot where it was left but that fails to remain in the sitting or down position, whichever is required by the particular exercise, until the handler has returned to the heel position, and a dog that repeatedly barks or whines, must receive less than 50 per cent of the available points. A substantial deduction shall be made for any dog that moves even a minor distance away from the place where it was left or that barks or whines only once or twice. Depending on the circumstances in each case, a substantial or minor deduction shall be made for touching the dog or for forcing it into the Down position. There shall be a minor deduction for sitting after the handler is in the heel position but before the judge has said 'Exercise finished' in the Down exercises. The dogs shall not be required to sit at the end of the Down exercises.

If a dog gets up and starts to roam or follows its handler, the judge shall promptly instruct the handler or one of the stewards to take the dog out of the ring or to keep it away from the other dogs. The judge should not attempt to judge the dogs or handlers on the manner in which they are made to Sit. The scoring of the Long Sit exercise will generally start after the judge has given the order 'Leave your dogs', except for such general things as rough

M

treatment of a dog by its handler or active resistance by a dog to its handler's attempts to make it Sit.

During these exercises the judge shall stand in such a position that all the dogs are in his line of vision, and where he can see all the handlers in the ring, or leaving and returning to the ring, without having to turn around.

SECTION 23   *Drop on Recall*   The orders for this exercise are the same as for the Recall, except that the dog is required to drop when coming in on command or signal from its handler when ordered by the judge, and except that an additional order or signal to 'Call your dog' is given by the judge after the Drop. The dog's prompt response to the handler's command or signal to Drop is a principal feature of this exercise, in addition to the prompt responses and the Stays as described under Recall above. A dog that does not stop and drop completely on a single command or signal must be scored zero. Minor or substantial deductions shall be made for a slow drop, depending on whether the dog is just short of perfection in this respect, or very slow in dropping, or somewhere between the two extremes. All other deductions as listed under Recall above shall also apply.

The judge may designate the point at which the handler is to give the command or signal to drop by some marker placed in advance which will be clear to the handler but not obvious to the dog, or he may give the handler a signal for the Drop, but such signal must be given in such a way as not to attract the dog's attention.

If a point is designated, the dog is still to be judged on its prompt response to the handler's command or signal rather than on its proximity to the designated point.

SECTION 24   *Retrieve on the Flat*   The orders for this exercise are 'Throw it,' 'Send your dog', 'Take it', 'Finish'. The principal feature of this exercise is to retrieve promptly. Any dog that fails to go out on the first command or a dog that fails to retrieve, shall be marked zero. A dog that goes to retrieve before the command or signal is given, or that does not return with the dumbbell sufficiently close so that the handler can readily take it without moving either foot or stretching forward, must receive less than 50 per cent of the points. Depending on the specific circumstances in each case, minor or substantial deductions shall be made for slowness in going out or returning or in picking up the dumbbell, mouthing or playing with the dumbbell, dropping the dumbbell, slowness in releasing the dumbbell to the handler, touching the handler on coming in, sitting between his feet, failure to sit in front or to Finish. Minor deductions shall be made for poor or slow Sits or Finishes.

SECTION 25 *Retrieve over High Jump* The orders for this exercise are 'Throw it', 'Send your dog', 'Take it', and 'Finish'. The principal features of this exercise are that the dog must go out over the jump, pick up the dumbbell and promptly return with it over the jump. The minimum penalties shall be the same as for the Retrieve on the Flat, and in addition a dog that fails both going and returning to go over the High Jump, must be marked zero. A dog that retrieves properly but goes over the High Jump in only one direction, must receive less than 50 per cent of the available points. Substantial deductions must be made for a dog that climbs the jump or uses the top of the jump for aid in going over, in contrast to a dog that merely touches the jump. Minor deductions shall be made for touching the jump in going over.

The jumps may be preset by the stewards based on the handler's advice as to the dog's height. The judge must make certain that the jump is set at the required height for each dog. He shall verify with an ordinary folding rule or steel tape to the nearest one-half inch, the height at the withers of each dog that jumps less than 36 inches. He shall not base his decision as to the height of the jump on the handler's advice.

SECTION 26 *Broad Jump* The orders for this exercise are 'Leave your dog', 'Send your dog', and 'Finish'. Any dog that refuses the jump on the first command or signal or walks over any part of the jump must be marked zero. A dog that fails to stay until the handler gives the command or signal to jump, or that fails to clear the full distance with its forelegs, shall receive less than 50 per cent of the available points. There shall be minor penalties for failure to return smartly to the handler and to sit straight in front of the handler or finish correctly, as in the Recall. It is the judge's responsibility to see that the distance jumped is that required by these Regulations for the particular dog.

SECTION 27 *Scent Discrimination* The orders for each of these two exercises are 'Send your dog', 'Take it', and 'Finish'. The principal features of these exercises are the selection of the handler's article from among the other articles by scent alone, and the prompt carrying of the right article to the handler after its selection. The minimum penalties shall be the same as for the Retrieve on the Flat and in addition a dog that fails to go out to the group of articles or that retrieves a wrong article, or that fails to bring the right article to the handler, must be marked zero for the particular exercise. Substantial deductions shall be made for a dog that picks up a wrong article, even though it puts it down again immediately, and for any roughness by the handler in imparting his scent to the dog. Minor or substantial deductions, depending on the circumstances in each case, shall be made for a dog that is slow or inattentive, or that does not work continuously. There shall be no penalty for a dog that takes a reasonably long time examining the articles, provided it is working smartly and continuously.

The judge shall select one article from each of the two sets and shall make written notes of the numbers of the two articles selected. The handler has the option as to which article he picks up first, but must give up each article immediately when ordered by the judge. The judge must see to it that the handler imparts his scent to the article only with his hands and that, between the time the handler picks up each article and the time he gives it to the judge, the article is held continuously in the handler's hands which must remain in plain sight. The judge or his steward must handle each of the eight other articles as he places them in the ring. The judge must make sure that they are properly separated before the dog is sent so that there may be no confusion of scent between articles.

SECTION 28 *Directed Retrieve* The orders for this exercise are 'Right', or 'Center', or 'Left', 'Take it' and 'Finish'. The principal features of this exercise are that the dog stay until directed to retrieve, that it go directly to the designated glove, and that it retrieve promptly. A dog that fails to go out on command or that fails to go directly in a straight line to the glove designated, or that fails to retrieve the glove, shall be marked zero. A dog that goes to retrieve before the command is given or that does not return promptly with the glove sufficiently close so that the handler can readily take it without moving either foot or stretching forward, must receive less than 50 per cent of the available points. Depending on the specific circumstances in each case, minor or substantial deductions shall be made for touching the dog or for excessive movements in getting it to heel facing the designated glove, for slowness or hesitation in going out or returning, or in picking up the glove, for mouthing or playing with the glove, for dropping the glove, for slowness in releasing it to the handler, and for failure to sit in front or to Finish. Minor deductions shall be made for poor or slow Sits or Finishes.

SECTION 29 *Signal Exercise* The orders for this exercise are 'Forward', 'Left turn', 'Right turn', 'About turn', 'Halt', 'Slow', 'Normal', 'Fast', 'Stand', and 'Leave your dog', and in addition the judge must give the handler signals to signal his dog to Drop, to Sit, to Come, to Finish. The orders for those parts of the exercise which are done with the dog at heel may be given in any order and may be repeated if necessary, except that the order to 'Stand' shall be given when the dog and handler are walking at a normal pace. The signals given the handler after he has left his dog in the Stand position shall be given in the order specified above. The principal feature of this exercise are the heeling of the dog and the Come on signal as described for the Heel and Recall exercises, and the prompt response to the other signals given to the dog at a distance. A dog that fails, on a single signal from the handler, to stand or remain standing where left, or to drop, or to sit and stay, or to come, or that receives a command or audible signal from the handler to do any of these parts of the exercise, shall receive less than 50 per cent of the available points. All of the deductions listed under the Heel and Recall exercises shall also apply to this exercise.

SECTION 30 *Directed Jumping* The judge's first order is 'Send your dog', then, after the dog has stopped at the far end of the ring, the judge shall designate which jump is to be taken by the dog, whereupon the handler commands and/or signals his dog to return to him over the designated jump, the dog sitting in front of the handler and finishing as in the Recall. After the dog returns to the handler the order 'Finish' is given followed by 'Exercise finished'. The same sequence is then followed for the other jump. The principal features of this exercise are that the dog goes away from the handler in the direction indicated, stops when commanded, jumps as directed, and returns as in the Recall.

A dog that, in either half of the exercise, anticipates the handler's command and/or signal to go out, that does not leave its handler, that does not go out between the jumps and a substantial distance beyond, that does not stop on command, that anticipates the handler's command and/or signal to jump, that does not jump as directed, or a dog that knocks the bar off the uprights or climbs over the High Jump or uses the top of the High Jump for aid in going over, must receive less than 50 per cent of the available marks. Substantial deductions shall be made for anticipating the Turn, Stop or Sit, and for failure to Sit. Substantial or minor deductions shall be made for faults such as slowness in going out or returning, slow response to direction, and poor sits or finishes, depending on the specific circumstances in each case.

The judge must make certain that the jumps are set at the required height for each dog by following the same procedure described for the Retrieve over High Jump.

SECTION 31 *Group Examination* The orders for this exercise are 'Stand your dogs', 'Leave your dogs', and 'Back to your dogs'. The principal features of this exercise are that the dog must stand and stay and must show no shyness nor resentment. A dog that moves a substantial distance away from the place where it was left, or that goes over to any other dog, or that sits or lies down before the handler returns to the heel position, or that growls or snaps at any time, must be marked zero. A dog that remains standing but that moves a minor distance away from the place where it was left, or a dog that shows any shyness or resentment or that repeatedly barks or whines, must receive less than 50 per cent of the available points. Depending on the specific circumstances in each case, minor or substantial deductions must be made for any dog that moves its feet at any time during the exercise, or sits or lies down after the handler has returned to the heel position. The judge should not attempt to judge the dogs or handlers on the manner in which the dogs are made to stand. The scoring will normally start after the judge has given the order 'Leave your dogs', except for such general things as rough treatment of a dog by its handler, or active resistance by a dog to its handler's attempts to make it stand. The dogs are not required to sit at the end of this exercise. The examination shall be conducted as in dog show judging, the judge going over each dog carefully with his hands. The judge must make a written record of any deductions immediately after examining each dog, subject to further deduction of points for subsequent faults. The judge must instruct one or more stewards to watch the other dogs while he conducts the individual examinations, and to call any faults to his attention.

SECTION 32 *Tracking Tests* For obvious reasons these tests cannot be held at a dog show, and a person, though he may be qualified to judge Obedience Trials, is not necessarily capable of judging a tracking test. He must be familiar with the various conditions that may exist when a dog is required to do nose work. Scent conditions, weather, lay of the land, etc., must be taken into consideration, and a thorough knowledge of this work is necessary.

One or both of the judges must personally lay out or walk over each track after it has been laid out, a day or so before the test, so as to be completely familiar with the location of the track, landmarks and ground conditions. At least two of the major turns shall be well out in the open country where there are no fences or other boundaries to guide the dog. No major part of any track shall follow along any fence or boundary within 15 yards of such boundary. The track shall include at least two right angle turns and should include more than two such turns so that the dog may be observed working in different wind directions. Acute angle turns should be avoided whenever possible. No conflicting tracks shall be laid. No track shall cross any body of water. No part of any track shall be laid within 75 yards of any other track. In the case of two tracks going in opposite directions, however, the first flags of these tracks may be as close as 50 yards from each other. The judges shall make sure that the track is no less than 440 yards and that the tracklayer is a stranger to the dog in each case. It is the judge's responsibility to instruct the tracklayer to insure that each track is properly laid and that each tracklayer carries a copy of the chart with him in laying the track. The judges must approve the article to be left at the end of each track and must see that it is thoroughly impregnated with the tracklayer's scent and that the tracklayer's shoes meet the requirements of these regulations.

There is no time limit provided the dog is working, but a dog that is off the track and is clearly not working should not be given any minimum time, but should be marked Failed. The handler may not be given any assistance by the judges or anyone else. If a dog is not trailing it shall not be marked Passed even though it may have found the article. In case of unforseen circumstances, the judges may in rare cases, at their own discretion, give a handler and his dog a second chance on a new track. A track for each dog entered shall be plotted on the ground not less than one day before the test, the track being marked by flags which the tracklayer can follow readily on the day of the test. A chart of each track shall be made up in duplicate, showing the approximate lengths in yards of each leg, and major landmarks and boundaries, if any. Two of these charts shall be marked, one by each of the judges, at the time the dog is tracking, so as to show the approximate course followed by the dog. The judges shall sign their charts and show on each whether the dog 'Passed' or 'Failed', the time the tracklayer started, the time the dog started and finished tracking, a brief description of ground, wind and weather conditions, the wind direction, and note of any steep hills or valleys.

Index